FINDING YOUR WAY

after

Your Spouse Dies

FINDING YOUR WAY

after

Your Spouse Dies

MARTA FELBER

ave maria press Notre Dame, Indiana

International Standard Book Number: 0-87793-932-2

Cover design by Brian C. Conley.

Text design by Katherine Robinson Coleman.

Printed and bound in the United States of America.

This book is dedicated to you, the reader, with the sincere hope that it will be of help in your journey through grief.

Sincere appreciation goes to my son, Karl Sandrock, who graciously gave of his time to be my "at-home" editor.

Six widowed persons met with me in a group experience bi-weekly for three months, reviewed all the first drafts of these chapters, and gave valuable feedback. My heartfelt thanks go to Leroy Anderson, Virginia Burdick, Sallye Cate, Evelyn Coelho, JoAnn Diercouff, and Ivo Mersmann.

Step by Step

Open the Door

Your spouse has died, and I'm sorry. How I wish that I could be with you in person. I would invite you to join me in a comfortable spot with a cup of coffee or tea. That is not possible, but, as you read through these pages, I hope that you will feel the warmth and encouragement that you might find in caring conversation with a friend.

I don't know exactly how you feel, but I care that you are hurting, and I think I may be able to offer you some help and some hope out of my own grief experiences. My journey through grief was some time ago, but I still remember much of what it was like. Of course, your grief is unique to you and not exactly like mine. But in the pages of this book, I think we may find some common feelings and needs.

It helped me tremendously to write things down— my feelings, problems, lists of things to do, measurements, and more. This book will be an even greater help if you come to it with pen and paper in hand; I strongly encourage you to locate a notebook that you might be able to make use of regularly.

My personal faith was also central in my journey. Of course, if I talk too much about my own faith, it may get in the way of your own spiritual expression. Let me just encourage you to deepen your faith and continually draw from it. At the end of each chapter, I have begun a prayer for you. I hope that you will continue praying, as long as you wish, before you say "Amen." The Old and New Testament scriptures are there for you to read, if and when you choose to do so.

Also, please check the list of resources at the end of this book, where I list several sources of additional help.

It is not my nature to give advice, so please take what I say as suggestions only. Use what works for you and let the rest go. Also keep in mind that there is no set schedule in this journey through grief. The important thing is to keep moving.

Dear God, Together we take your hand and ask you to join us in our journey through grief. We know that you won't turn loose. Help us to hold on to you. . . . Amen.

SCRIPTURE PASSAGES FOR REFLECTION

ISAIAH 43:1-3A

MATTHEW 7:7, 8

Create Your Own "Comfort Place"

I have what I call a comfort "cozy": an afghan that my favorite aunt lovingly made for me. Yours might be a family quilt, a warm blanket, an enveloping coat that belonged to your loved one. Choose a spot in your home to claim as your "comfort place"—an easy chair that you normally don't use or your loved one's special chair—and spread your comfort cozy there, ready to surround you when you sit down.

Go to this special place when you want to cry, or to just sit quietly and think about your loved one. Pull your comfort cozy around you. Feel its warmth and protection. Try curling into a ball. Talk aloud, if that feels right. Listen for what your loved one may be saying to you. Share your experiences and your longings. What is bothering you? What is hardest for you to bear? Maybe anger and guilt could be worked out here. Express your thoughts and feelings, whatever they are, and then let them go. Feel your loved one's love. Feel God's love. Hold on to both.

Stay as long as you wish in your comfort place. Stretch a little, and leave only when you are ready.

You will have need for your comfort place in the days and weeks ahead. It is always there, your refuge in the storm. If you are away from home when grief starts to overwhelm you, remember that your comfort place is there, waiting.

Dear God, You are allowed and welcome in my special grieving spot. You are with me always, but let me feel your comforting arms even closer in my comfort place. Draw me nearer. . . . Amen.

SCRIPTURE PASSAGES FOR REFLECTION

PSALM 18:1, 2

MARK 4:35-41

Build a Support Network

Have you ever written something to remember on the palm of your hand in order to make sure that you won't forget? I have. If you were to reach out your palm right now, I would write, "Get emotional support!" That, I believe, is your single most important task as you journey through grief.

Family and friends may be sympathetic and understanding to the outpouring of your feelings. On the other hand, they may not. They may be too submerged in their own grief. The death of your loved one may be perceived as a threat to their own mortality. Perhaps they are too involved in their own lives and problems, or perhaps they have simply never experienced a deep loss.

If family and friends fail, where do you look for the emotional support you must have? Find other persons who are also mourning the loss of a loved one. They will understand. Search in your faith community, in grief support groups, or at community agencies. It helped me tremendously that I had new widow friends who were at different stages in their grief. Foster a relationship with these empathetic persons. Spend time together. Call each other. The support needs to be ongoing and mutually fulfilling.

Make a list of all your other support needs and look for individuals who can help. I still have the list that I began in those early months when I found myself alone. Some of my categories were repair (home and car), companionship, financial, medical, legal, home maintenance, problem-solving. You will think of more. Get referrals from people you know, and continue to maintain your list.

It can be hard to ask for help, but remember that you are responsible for getting the support you must have.

Dear God, Many times I have failed to call on you in my need. You are at the top of my support list. I know that your sustaining love is always there for me. . . . Amen.

SCRIPTURE PASSAGES FOR REFLECTION

PSALM 121

1 JOHN 4:13-16

Accept
the Crying

God created us with tear ducts. What a wonderful invention! Tears wash out impurities and lubricate our eyes. God also gives us the capacity for feeling the grief that triggers tears; surely that means the Creator expects, even wants, us to cry.

For many of us, this is difficult; we feel embarrassed when we cry. From somewhere we got the erroneous idea that tears show weakness. This is simply not true. Tears of grief are evidence that we have the courage to cry, the courage to show our grief in this way. The crying-in-public time won't last forever; it just seems that way when we can't stop crying when we think we should. Say to yourself, "It's okay for me to show my grief; it's okay for me to cry." Remember, when we lose something that's not valuable, we don't cry!

There were times when I would feel my sorrow building up, but could not release it. I learned to do certain things to open the floodgate. Sometimes I would get a photo album, packets of our pictures, or mementos I had saved. Reading cards that my loved one had given me or touching or holding his clothing close to me often allowed the tears to come. The more I could bring on these crying times when I was alone, the less often I felt out of control and cried in public.

Tears can be healthy and healing, whether they are shed publicly in the early months or—during those gully-washing crying times—alone or with close family and friends.

Dear God, Thank you for providing tears as a way of release for my grief. I know that you feel and accept my tears whenever and wherever I cry. You have promised never to leave me comfortless. I claim that promise now. . . . Amen.

SCRIPTURE PASSAGES FOR REFLECTION

PSALM 56:8, 12, 13

JOHN 11:33-35

Ask for a Hug

"Have you hugged your grieving friend today?" Now there's a bumper sticker that a lot of people would benefit from! People in grief are usually starving to be held in a warm embrace. Hugs may come in the early days of grief, as an acceptable expression of caring. But, like the cards and calls that dwindle away, the hugs may also disappear.

It is up to you to meet your hug quota for the day! When your friend asks, "How are you today?" you might reply, "I'd feel better if I had a hug." Or, simply, "I need a hug," and welcome it. If you know that someone is not comfortable with hugging, you could simply reach out your hand for the touch of another hand in yours.

With your closest friends, don't hesitate to say, "I need to be held." Relax into those arms. Cry if you feel like it. Keep those feelings of being encircled, to recall when alone. You may even need to schedule these times with someone who cares enough to hold you.

Don't overlook the love that children can offer. Bend down to a child's level, one who is your friend, and tell them the truth: "I'd like a hug; will you give me one?" Hugs from children are hugs from the heart, so treasure them. Repeat each time you see this child, "Remember, I always need a hug, and your hugs are great!"

When all else fails, hug yourself. Yes, I mean literally. Stop right now and practice. One arm feels more natural crossed over the other. Find which one. Reach up so each hand is grabbing an upper arm or shoulder, whichever feels better. Now squeeze and hold. Feed yourself a positive message, like "You're going to make it!"

Make sure you get at least one hug a day, and remember: the more, the better!

Dear God, I don't need to ask for your encircling arms to be around me. I just need to feel them, as I do now. . . . Amen.

SCRIPTURE PASSAGES FOR REFLECTION

ISAIAH 40:11

JOHN 15:9-17

Deepen Your Faith

The blow you were dealt when your loved one died may have thrown you off the rock of your faith. At this point, you may feel as if you're hanging on with one hand and with the other shaking your fist and screaming "Why?" Please know that it is okay to voice anger toward God; God can handle it. Also find someone to listen to your feelings who will understand. With help, you can slowly but surely climb back to a secure spot on your rock of faith.

What might help you to do this?

Schedule a time every day for meditation, prayer, and reading. Let nothing interfere. Then sit in absolute stillness, allowing yourself to be open to what God might have to say. Snatch moments of quiet throughout the day to breathe a prayer and touch your faith.

There are people reaching out to you from the rock of faith. Join them, individually and when they gather together. Feel the power of combined faith. Meet with your priest or pastor, or with someone else whom you trust as a spiritual advisor. They have much to offer you. Ask questions; share your doubts and fears. Allow them to hear your grief and feel your pain.

Join in spiritual retreats. There is nothing quite like drawing apart from all the busyness of the world and dealing with the deepest issues of life. Or plan a retreat of your own, designed to meet your personal needs.

Some people find renewal of their faith in writing. Choose a beautifully bound notebook and begin "My Personal Faith Journal." Write about your longings and aspirations. Formulate your beliefs. On paper or in your mind, finish the sentence, "My faith promises. . . ." Make a list and continue to add to your beliefs. Center yourself on these assurances of your faith, making your position on the rock more secure.

Dear God, Be patient with my wanderings, my doubts, and my fears. Give me the strength to return. . . . Amen.

SCRIPTURE PASSAGES FOR REFLECTION

PSALM 40:1-5

HEBREWS 11:1-3

Recognize Denial

My denial began in the hospital. "The doctors will find out what is wrong with him, and he will be well again," I told myself. And yet he died, as they said he would. When did your denial begin? Most of us don't talk about death in our everyday lives. Why should we, when everything is going fine? We try not to think about, or talk about, what is not.

But now, a terrible reality has broken into your life. Maybe your loved one was ill for a long time, or perhaps death was sudden, or even violent. Whatever the circumstances, nothing prepared you for that last breath. And when it happened, perhaps you found yourself saying, "It really isn't true."

There is a period, be it long or short, when we know in our head that our loved one is gone, but in our heart we still say, "It can't be!" Perhaps this denial allows us to get through the rituals, outpourings of sympathy, forms, and whatever else must be accomplished and endured. We may leave our loved one's voice on the answering machine or keep both names on joint financial accounts. We may think, "I will never take off my wedding ring." Perhaps we see our loved one in the stranger on the street or expect our loved one's step at the door. In the early period of grief, when these "it-isn't-true" thoughts arise, be kind to yourself. You are doing the best that you can. You will be able to deal with reality—later.

Dear God, It's just too much for me right now. I want my loved one back, by my side. Just for a little while, I need to deny that my loved one is gone. I promise to face reality later, when I can. I know you understand. I know you will help me. . . . Amen.

SCRIPTURE PASSAGES FOR REFLECTION

1 SAMUEL 16:7

1 PETER 5:6-7

Start
a Journal

It began in the hospital room where my loved one was dying—the outpouring of my feelings on paper. Sometimes the words wrote themselves, so urgent was the need for expression! Parts were difficult to read later—where tears had mingled with the words, and yet, journal writing was the most helpful thing I did in my journey through grief.

Are you writing your thoughts and feelings? If not, I urge you to begin. A spiral notebook works well. Keep it in a special place, where it is easily accessible. Write whatever enters your mind. Put the date and time before each entry, to cast it in reality. Write only for yourself—although you can always choose to share parts of your journal later.

Worries can get stuck, going around and around in your head, with no escape. Writing them down can allow you to let go of these anxious thoughts. Also take time to write about the good things. There are times when you have taken control, jobs you have completed. Record any progress you have made, however small. A problem you can't solve? Put it here, leave it, and come back later—perhaps to find an answer waiting for you. Friends are not accessible at every moment. Your journal can be your "instant friend," always there to "hear" your grief, your pain, your plans.

Finally, writing in your journal is a good way to close the day. What happened today? How did I feel? What was the worst today? The best? Is there something I want to remember for tomorrow? Something I need to do? Write it all down, and feel the release that writing can give.

Dear God, Even closer than my journal, you are with me always. You are reading over my shoulder as I pour out my thoughts and feelings. Accept these outpourings as part of me. I rest myself in you. . . . Amen.

SCRIPTURE PASSAGES FOR REFLECTION

PSALM 55:22

ROMANS 5:1-5

Benefit From Meditation

You no doubt already have many practices which you have made an essential part of your day; no one has to tell you to brush your teeth! Meditation is not as familiar to many of us, but it can become just as essential and routine. We are told that the benefits of meditation are abundant. It can help relieve tension and stress, pain and physical ailments, anxiety and depression. It energizes the body and the mind. Problems are faced with more clarity and focus. Why not give it a three-month trial? (Research says that this is the time period needed to firmly establish a habit.)

Choose a time when you are least likely to be disturbed. Take the phone off the hook or put on the answering machine. Sit or lie down. Close your eyes. Begin to relax your entire body. Think about each muscle in your face relaxing—your forehead, eyelids, cheeks, lips, and jaw. Continue down your body in this manner. Then check to make sure no muscle in your entire body is still tense. If there is one, relax it.

Breathe deeply, and when you breathe out say the word or phrase that you have chosen, aloud or silently. Some suggested words are "One," "God," and "Love." I use "Peace" as mine. It is to be uttered each time you breathe out. As thoughts come, and they will, tell yourself you will deal with them later. Then return your focus to breathing and the word you have chosen. Start with three to five minutes and gradually extend your meditation time. Twenty minutes, once or twice a day, is recommended.

End your meditation slowly, waiting a few moments to open your eyes. Then gently stretch. Wiggle your fingers and toes. Take with you the feelings of quietness and peace as you get to your feet and resume your day.

Dear God, Help me to center the mind that you gave me. May I feel your peace that passes all understanding and take it with me throughout my day. . . . Amen.

SCRIPTURE PASSAGES FOR REFLECTION

PSALM 42

LUKE 5:15, 16

Schedule a
Physical Check-Up

If you were contemplating a long and arduous motor trip, over rough terrain, you would certainly schedule a tune-up for your car. Why not do the same for yourself? The journey through grief can be long and rough: the illness and death of a loved one, with its accompanying sorrow, takes a physical toll, and the immune system may be weakened. Your body needs all the help you can give it.

Schedule a physical exam and visit with your doctor. He or she needs to know if your loved one's illness was long and painful or if the death was traumatic. Describe exactly how you have felt, both physically and emotionally. The emotional stress of grief may cause physical conditions to develop. These need to be identified and treated. Getting a thorough physical examination can put your mind to rest about any feared diseases, including any that your loved one may have had.

Be cautious, however, when tranquilizers and sleeping medications are prescribed. An important part of the grieving process is being in touch with feelings and expressing them. Some medications can deaden emotions. While this may bring relief for the moment, it does postpone the resolution of grief.

Taken over a long period, sleeping pills may become addictive. If your doctor prescribes these types of medications, voice your concerns and discuss the possibility of monitored short-term use.

Physical movement offers many benefits to the person in grief. With your doctor, devise an exercise program appropriate for you. Have clear guidelines for how and when to increase your exercise level.

Dear God, Give me the physical strength and healing I need. At the same time, may I feel your healing touch for my wounded soul. . . . Amen.

SCRIPTURE PASSAGES FOR REFLECTION

JEREMIAH 30:17A

3 JOHN 2-4

Walk Each Day

"If only I could sleep at night. . . ." "I'm so depressed." The majority of widowed persons have these complaints. Luckily, there is a non-drug prescription that could help relieve both these conditions: take a short walk each day, starting today. Slowly increase the number of walks per day and the speed, as you are able.

Why walk? It is one of the best forms of exercise. Most people can do it. No special equipment is needed, except properly fitting shoes with adequate support. Walking improves the body, reduces stress, and restores the soul. It provides a much-needed time-out from grief.

We tend to stick with an exercise program that we enjoy, so find what would make walking a pleasure for you. Try communing with nature as you walk. People-watch. Listen to music or books on tape, if it is safe where you walk to do this. Plan your day or set short-term goals. Sort out problems or do the opposite and go into a "mindless mode." A walking buddy might be the answer. Find what fits you.

Choose places to walk that are safe. Mall-walking has become so popular that now many malls even encourage it, making the main concourses of the mall available even before individual stores open for business.

Many people prefer to walk early in the day. Others walk after a meal. There are those who walk the dog. Establish your walking habit and feel your spirits lift!

Dear God, As I walk in your world help me to be more aware of all your creation, including people. May my walking be a form of worship. . . . Amen.

SCRIPTURE PASSAGES FOR REFLECTION

PSALM 8

ACTS 17:24-28

Eat Regularly and Well

As you work through grief, you may not care what or when you eat or if you eat at all. It may even be hard for you to swallow when you do eat. Mealtimes can be sharp reminders of loneliness. In my own early period of grief, I could not eat in the dining area and face my loved one's empty chair. So I created an eating place in the kitchen. Sometimes I ate on a tray and watched TV. Many breakfasts I ate in bed. However you accomplish it, the important thing is to eat—regularly and well.

Can you hear the voice of your mother? "Come on, dear, you've got to eat something. It will make you strong! Just try a little. That's right."

Listen to the voice of your friend: "Let's go to lunch today. We'll stop for groceries on the way home and stock your refrigerator and shelves."

Remember the advice of nutritionists: "Every day we need to eat fruits, vegetables, whole grains, low-fat dairy products, and a small amount of protein."

Don't forget the help you can find in your local bookstore: "We have a cookbook that focuses on easy-to-fix healthy meals."

Consider the advice of your doctor: "Take a multivitamin and mineral supplement every day, just to be sure you get your nutrients."

Finally, keep in mind what your loved one might say: "You know that I want you to eat and be healthy. If you can't do it for yourself, do it for me."

Dear God, Can it be that you are really concerned about my eating well? I hear you saying that my body is the temple of God. Help me to see my body as sacred and that it needs to be nourished with good food. But feed my soul as well, as only you can. . . . Amen.

SCRIPTURE PASSAGES FOR REFLECTION

PSALM 145:14-21

1 CORINTHIANS 6:19, 20

Appreciate the Straight Stretches

This journey through grief is not a smooth highway with clearly marked signs and exits. It is an unpaved and unknown road. There are bumps, ruts, hills, curves, and even detours. Enjoy any straight stretch, but be aware—there are curves ahead!

The first time that I really laughed after my loved one died was at a play, "Nunsense." Once I got started laughing I couldn't stop—one belly laugh after another. Others around me were laughing almost as much. It felt unbelievably good! But, when I got home, I sank into depression. Guilty feelings erased the laughter. How could I let myself have so much fun when my loved one was dead? Up and down! I had gone from joyful abandonment to the depth of depression in just a few short hours.

You will experience moments of joy, fulfillment, even contentment in the days ahead. Perhaps you will be surprised when this happens. Snatch these moments, treasure them, and hold them close to you as long as you can. Don't let guilt take them away, as I did. You deserve to feel happy again. Your loved one would want this for you. Allow, even plan for, these enjoyable, fulfilling new experiences. Put these snatched moments in your memory storehouse, to bring out when the road gets rough again.

Dear God, You are walking down this journey of grief, just ahead of me. You know the road. You will be there when I need you to help me over the bumps. Be my constant guide. Lead me. . . . Amen.

SCRIPTURE PASSAGES FOR REFLECTION

PSALM 23

ROMANS 8:37-39

Organize for Early Tasks

It is the rare widowed person who has everything in order, who has a plan in place for what he or she will do when his or her loved one dies. Most of us are scrambling for important papers, trying to handle a hundred details, when that is the last thing in the world we want to do or feel we can do.

You need a master list of what must be done immediately and how, and another list with plans for the first month or so. A lawyer, preferably one who is knowledgeable in matters of estate, is your best bet to help with this. If you don't know such a lawyer, get a referral from friends or the local bar association. If finances are a problem, check with the bar association for local "pro bono" or legal services lawyers.

A large spiral notebook is ideal for keeping track of all you need to do. Check off accomplished tasks. Consider an accordion cardboard file for keeping together all the necessary documents and papers. Choose a time to work on these have-to jobs when you are feeling more "up" and able to concentrate better. If you can, ask a friend who is adept at business matters to give you ongoing help with these tasks.

When you get your mail, don't be tempted simply to rifle through it and then pile it somewhere. These piles grow! My strategy for mail was as follows: Junk mail was tossed immediately. Cards and letters of condolence were put in a basket, to be read at times when needed most. Bills and letters requiring an answer went into a special drawer, to be dealt with on the first and middle of each month.

As you are able, design similar strategies for yourself and, slowly, you will be able to make it through the details that may now seem overwhelming.

Dear God, I think of the order and purpose in your creation. Help me to create some order in my confused world and to complete the necessary tasks. . . . Amen.

SCRIPTURE PASSAGES FOR REFLECTION

PSALM 147:1-18

2 TIMOTHY 1:7

Prepare for the Night

The sleepless nights in the early period of grief seem endless! You may find it difficult to get to sleep, you may wake and find it difficult to get back to sleep, or you may wake up too early. Will it help if I tell you that this interrupted sleep pattern is normal and will eventually correct itself? "Yes," you may say, "but what can I do now?"

Getting ready for the night begins during the day! Schedule vigorous exercise every morning or early afternoon (but not in the evening, when you need to wind down). If you do take a nap during the day, set a timer and allow thirty minutes or less. Avoid caffeine and alcohol for four to six hours before bedtime. If worries or fears are nagging, share them with a friend or deal with them yourself. Leave them outside your bedroom.

Perhaps most important is to develop a before-bedtime routine that takes thirty minutes or more. Be sure to include a spiritual routine as well as self-care. Begin at a set time and do the same thing every night in the same order. This signals to your body that sleep is approaching. If you normally get hungry at night, try a small glass of milk or a slice of turkey, which may help you get to sleep. Some people find a bath relaxing, but make sure the temperature is warm, not hot. Most people sleep better when the room is cool. If you tend to wake during the night and can't get back to sleep, you might have ready a radio tuned to a late-night talk show or a cassette player with a relaxing music tape ready to play. Make sure that the last things on your nightly routine are things that truly relax you—a little light reading, a relaxation exercise, or prayer and meditation time. This done, turn out the light, hold your loved one's pillow, and go to sleep.

Dear God, As a camel kneels every night to have its burden lifted off, I kneel before you. Take my burden of grief. Let me rest in your encircling arms. . . . Amen.

SCRIPTURE PASSAGES FOR REFLECTION

PSALM 63:1-8

PHILIPPIANS 4:6, 7

Greet the Day

The optimist wakes up and says, "Good morning, God," while the pessimist growls, "Good God—morning!" Are you more like the pessimist, not wanting to face your days? "What is there to live for?" you may ask, and then pull the sheet over your head and try to go back to sleep. You may reach out to an empty bed and start to cry. Or do you begin mulling over what you don't want to do that day, but think you must?

Resolve that tomorrow's "wake-up call" be different. Choose a sentence or phrase to program into your inner alarm clock. Have it come on automatically in those hazy moments when you are not quite awake, but neither are you fully asleep. It might be something like "God is with me," "I am at peace," or "I count my blessings." Choose words that will start your day off right, to say over and over before you open your eyes.

Then stretch and yawn, slowly, like a cat or a dog waking from sleep. Push against the headboard and lengthen your body. Hold, relax, and stretch again. Pull one knee up toward your chest and hold. Relax. Repeat with the other leg. Beginning with your face and continuing to your toes, tense every muscle in your body. Really tense, hold, and then release completely. If that feels good, repeat. Include your own stretches.

Slip out of bed and head for the kitchen and a steaming cup of tea or coffee. Select from the shelf a cup or mug to keep just for this first beverage of the day. Fill it and move to your morning meditation spot. Direct your thoughts and prayers in a positive and thankful direction. Read inspirational passages. Plan something pleasant to do. Think of someone who needs your help. Then head for that healthy, but tasty breakfast!

Good morning, God, Thank you for this new day to live and work in your world. Continue to be with me and guide me today and every day. . . . Amen.

SCRIPTURE PASSAGES FOR REFLECTION

PSALM 30:4, 5

EPHESIANS 1:3-6

Ignore Certain Messages

Watch out: you may find yourself receiving messages about grieving from society, from people you know, or even from yourself that are not true. Whether explicitly or implicitly, you may be told the following:

* "Time will heal." (Time within itself will not heal. It is what you do with the time that will enable you to heal.)

* "If you start crying, you may not be able to stop." (You will stop crying. No one has kept on crying forever!)

* "You need to keep busy to help you forget." (Going through grief means remembering, feeling, and then releasing. This takes time.)

* "People who have faith in God don't have to grieve the death of a loved one." (God understands and grieves along with us.)

* "If you have fun, you are being disrespectful to your loved one." (Finding joy again in living is a tribute to your loved one. It is what you deserve.)

* "A widowed person is a threat to their friends' marriages." (If you have no designs on their mate, then this is only true in their minds and is their problem.)

* "You should be back to normal by now." (No two grief experiences are the same. You are a unique person and need to grieve in your own way, in your own time. Also, you can never return to "normal." You are building a new life.)

* "Be strong for the children." (Your children need to see some of your grief. It gives them permission to show and share theirs. Allowing yourself times for pouring out your grief with supportive friends will free you to be a more supportive parent.)

* "I will avoid pain by not grieving." (Perhaps the worst pain comes by holding in grief. Share your grief with others who care.)

Dear God, Help me to find my own path through grief, knowing that you are with me, every step of the way. . . . Amen.

SCRIPTURE PASSAGES FOR REFLECTION

PSALM 43:3-5

JAMES 1:5-7

Give Positive Feedback

You have only one person with you every day, twenty-four hours a day: yourself! And whether you realize it or not, you are constantly talking to yourself. Are you critical? ("That was a stupid thing to do!") Or are you nurturing? ("I understand why you forgot the appointment.") If you were to balance the number of positive comments against the negatives in this internal monologue, on which side would the scales tip?

Most of us dish out more put-downs to ourselves than we realize. They come so easily! Perhaps you were told "you are not okay" in one way or another when you were a child. These messages are still with you. Now, they must be counterbalanced with positive messages. You are the one to do this. Maybe you were taught not to think highly of yourself. Give yourself permission to look for and validate your positive attributes and your successes. You can speak as a nurturing parent to yourself, even if you did not have one in real life.

You also need to catch yourself being negative about yourself. When you hear one of these messages, pause and focus your attention on what you are saying to yourself. Awareness is the first step in change. Let your nurturing parent rephrase that

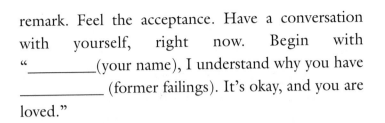

remark. Feel the acceptance. Have a conversation with yourself, right now. Begin with "_____(your name), I understand why you have _____ (former failings). It's okay, and you are loved."

Dear God, Your messages to me are always nurturing. Help me to feel and accept your unconditional love. Accept my attempts to make it through this difficult time. Thank you for always being there and loving me. . . . Amen.

SCRIPTURE PASSAGES FOR REFLECTION

PSALM 103:1-5

JOHN 3:14-16

Postpone Some Decisions

Are you feeling overwhelmed by all the decisions to be made and things to get done? Find your notebook. Take three pages and write at the top of the first, "Do Now," on the second, "Do Later," and on the third, "Do Whenever." Next, list all the decisions facing you and all the tasks waiting to be accomplished, putting each on one of the three pages and leaving spaces to make notes. Now go back to the first page. Beside each "Now" item, make notes as to how and when you will do that specific thing, including the name of a person who might help. Use this as your work plan. Cross off each item as you take care of it, and feel good about yourself.

From time to time you will need to add to page one, or move items from "Do Later" to "Do Now." But you can handle them, one at a time. Don't let anyone pressure you into doing anything before you are ready. You may get lots of advice. "You should move from your house. It's too big for you, and you have too many memories there." "Why don't you get a new car? You'll be more comfortable." "Move your funds out of CDs and put them into stocks. That's where you make money." These statements may be true, but far-reaching decisions need to be made later, if possible. Take your time. Wait until you can become knowledgeable about the decisions you need to make. Find wise, objective persons to help you make important decisions when the time is right. Listen, evaluate their counsel, then choose what is best for you. The early months of grief need to be kept for grieving and not for making big changes.

Dear God, Keep me from moving too fast in making decisions. I pray the Serenity Prayer: "God, grant me the serenity to accept the things I cannot change, the courage to change the things I can, and the wisdom to know the difference." . . . Amen.

SCRIPTURE PASSAGES FOR REFLECTION

ISAIAH 30:19-21

COLOSSIANS 3:17

Get a Grip on Finances

Regretfully, we do have to deal with money, sometimes in the earliest stages of grief. As soon as you are able, contact trusted professionals to help you with the decisions you must make. Ask for clarification if you do not understand. Make copious notes in your notebook. Review the facts, figures, and directives with each person, making sure they are correct. Some possible contacts: a bank representative, your insurance companies, the Social Security office, your financial broker, a financial advisor, your loved one's employer, and a CPA.

One of the first steps is to get a good sense of your financial position. Using your collected information, determine your assets. Then list your debts, estimating where you do not have the figures. Subtract the two sums. This will give you an idea of where you stand financially and if you will need help.

"Budget" is often considered a dirty word. A simple monthly budget, however, can offer you a sense of security. If this is the first time you have worked with a budget, you may want to keep it very simple: itemize your fixed expenses and estimate other costs of living, allowing a sum for unforeseen expenditures. Later you may want to create a more detailed and precise budget.

Remember that many financial matters can wait. Medical bills, for example, should be kept in a safe place until all insurance companies have paid their share. In my case, that took seven months! If you don't need the cash immediately, hold acceptance of insurance and company benefits until you have time to decide in what form you want the payments. Invest funds only after having made yourself knowledgeable. Do not be pressured into hasty decisions.

The Widowed Persons Service, a program of the AARP, conducts financial planning workshops, open to widowed persons of any age, and there are excellent books providing financial know-how. Take advantage of all the help that is available.

Dear God, My mind is so muddled that I find it difficult to deal with all these money matters. Grant me clear thinking to make assessments and wise decisions. . . . Amen.

SCRIPTURE PASSAGES FOR REFLECTION

MALACHI 3:10-12

MATTHEW 6:19-21

Get Off the Treadmill

Time seemed to stand still when my loved one died. Every day was the same as the day before. It felt as if I were on a treadmill, not getting off, and going nowhere. Endless. And yet I had to keep walking.

Maybe you feel the same way? Make something happen to change your day. Plan it the night before and write a note to yourself, putting it where you will see it first thing in the morning.

The list below can help get you started.

* Plan to wear something bright, colorful, or outlandish tomorrow.

* Think of a person to call with whom you have not talked in a long time, maybe someone who has moved away.

* Plan to eat one of your meals in an entirely different place. How about outside or in bed?

* If you always prepare your own food, try take-out.

* If you walk, take a direction that is new to you. You may have to drive, park, and then walk.

* Buy a present for yourself, something you don't really need but would like to have.

* Go to the library. Look at a magazine you have never read before. Check out a different kind of book.

- Call a family member and weave "I love you" into the conversation.
- Drop by your place of worship for a period of meditation and prayer.
- Take an aimless drive; discover something new.

Dear God, Lift me off my go-nowhere treadmill. Help me come alive to new possibilities. Help me feel good about even tiny changes in my day. . . . Amen.

SCRIPTURE PASSAGES FOR REFLECTION

PSALM 139:17, 18

2 CORINTHIANS 5:17

Assume Control

You had no choice when your loved one died. You were not in a position of control. Tears surfaced without bidding. Others around you may have taken over by instructing you to "do this; do that." Maybe you did not even care what got done. Now, you may have a lingering feeling of not being in control of your own life. Slowly, you need to regain that sense of control.

I strongly suggest that you put it all down in writing. Find a calendar with big spaces to write in. Whenever you do something for which you are responsible, note it on the calendar. No deed is too small. Notations can be as simple as: "Fixed loose drawer pull." "Remembered friend's birthday." "Wrote overdue letter."

Begin to say "I choose" to yourself before you perform any task. "I choose to take a walk." "I choose to clean out a drawer." "I choose to pay the bills this morning." "I choose to treat myself to a new book." "I choose to look at pictures and cry."

Choosing not to do something is also a choice and gives evidence of control. "I choose not to eat that second piece of cake." "I choose not to work on the accounting today." "I choose not to be upset that my friend forgot to call."

Each night look at what you did that day. Say to yourself, "Today I was able to. . . ." Even if you managed only one thing, celebrate that one thing. Begin to say to yourself: "I will do that, and then I can put it on my calendar." Then do it. Before you tear off from the calendar the month that has ended, read all of it again. Begin a new month, a little more in control.

Dear God, It is important that I do what I can to take control of my life. But, when I can't quite make it on my own, I know that you are there as my back-up! . . . Amen.

SCRIPTURE PASSAGES FOR REFLECTION

PSALM 33:20-22

2 TIMOTHY 2:15

Make Home Yours

Do you feel at home in your own house? Early in my grief, I dreaded facing the loneliness in my home and all the reminders of my loved one. Slowly and carefully, I began to make changes. You can too, when it feels right for you.

Start with one room or area. Sit quietly and look around. What reminders of your loved one do you see? What do you want to keep? What adaptations would make this room more comfortable for your lifestyle? Make a list of what you might change to make it more livable for you. Move to the next room and continue in this manner.

Begin with the easiest things to do on your lists. It is important to get started. It could be as simple a change as moving a plant to an empty spot where it would be in your view more throughout the day. What about finding a new cover for your bed? The moment you make one change, however simple, you are making your home yours.

It may be difficult for you to make changes in the spot which especially "belonged" to your loved one. If so, begin with small changes. For example, picture yourself sitting where your loved one always sat to watch TV, if that is a more convenient viewing spot for you. Then try sitting there. Over time, could you feel comfortable with this change?

Be willing to experiment. Your loved one does not physically live in your home anymore, and so objects and places used by your loved one are no longer needed. Your loved one's spirit remains, but it is not confined to a chair. Move, adapt, and add. Slowly, you can make your home yours.

Dear God, This is my physical home, for which I am thankful. But I am even more grateful for my spiritual home with you. It never changes. . . . Amen.

SCRIPTURE PASSAGES FOR REFLECTION

PSALM 84:1-4

HEBREWS 3:1-6

Visualize and Plan Ahead

The first time I went to a play alone, I didn't last through the first act. I got up and practically ran out of the theater to my car, where I burst into tears. In no way was I prepared for the emotions that swept over me as I sat down in that theater alone. In error I had thought, "It will do me good to get out. I've always enjoyed plays." But so had my loved one. We had seen many plays together, discussing them afterward. When I did go again, I took an understanding friend.

As you think ahead to any activity, celebration, anniversary that you shared, visualize how it might be without your loved one. Play the scene several ways. Only after you have done this, begin to plan what you can handle and how. You may choose to run. The first Christmas without my loved one, I did just that—I traveled to another place, knowing that I could not stay alone in what was our "Christmas home." You may choose to make smaller changes. If you bear the responsibility for other family members, include them in your visualization and then make plans together.

Your everyday pain will be intensified on anniversaries and special days. Make a special effort to plan how you might take care of yourself at those times. Schedule periods for rest and meditation, treats for yourself, time with a caring friend.

Dear God, I know that the anniversaries and celebrations ahead will be difficult without my loved one. Help me to visualize the future and plan wisely. Let me feel your Presence always near, before and during these times. . . . Amen.

SCRIPTURE PASSAGES FOR REFLECTION

JEREMIAH 29:11-13

ROMANS 8:26-30

Prepare for Celebrations

My loved one died on January 25. Almost immediately, I began to dread the next Christmas without him, exactly eleven months away! If only I could have reassured myself that, closer to that date, I would develop a plan to survive the celebration.

There are several suggestions you may want to keep in mind as you prepare for those "special days." First, decide what is important about the anniversary or celebration that is ahead. Write it down. Your work page for getting through the celebration may have headings like "Keep," "Get Rid Of," and "Add." Give yourself permission to do things differently, without any feelings of guilt. Talk things over with any other persons who must be included. Help them to understand your needs and feelings. Consider theirs as well. The important thing is to do this early, especially if you begin to feel anxious. It is a good idea to develop a "Plan B," in case circumstances change. Once your work is done, relax. Say to yourself, "I have a plan for that celebration. I can handle it."

Try to have reasonable expectations. There are important ways in which celebrations will not, and cannot, ever be the same again. So it is okay to plan for them to be different. Be realistic about what you can handle, both physically and emotionally. Be kind to yourself and nurturing. Get plenty of rest and don't attempt too much. Provide safe times and places to grieve.

Each celebration you survive will help you be stronger to face the next. Getting through each one means that "first-year anniversary" will never occur again. Slowly, you will be able to find joy in these celebrations again.

Dear God, How am I going to get through the celebration ahead without my loved one, who made it worth celebrating? Accept my fears and reservations, as I now tell them to you. I feel so alone and lonely! Take my hand and guide me. . . . Amen.

SCRIPTURE PASSAGES FOR REFLECTION

PSALM 31:3-5

JOHN 15:4-7

Comfort Your Younger Children

You may already know better than I do that when you have children in your home, your grief is twice as hard. Your children will have many of the same feelings as you do, but they will express those feelings in different ways, depending on age and maturity. It is important to assure them that they are not to blame. They may act out their misery and frustration or withdraw completely.

Make sure that they know that you are available to listen and to talk. Take time to probe (very gently!) their thoughts and feelings. All children have some concept of death—based on the death of a pet, death in friends' families, TV, etc. Help them with misconceptions. Hear their fears and answer their questions with words and images they can understand.

Don't be afraid to let your children see you cry at times. Cry together, and provide some opportunities to remember the loved one. Give as many hugs as allowed. Let them feel whatever strength you can muster. Children desperately need acceptance and security. Assure them that they will be taken care of, that the family will go on, and that they are part of it. Return to normal schedules as soon as possible. Most important is that you allow them their feelings and reassure them in the ways that you can.

As you work through your grief together, keep in mind that there are excellent resources to guide you, including those listed on pages 138-151.

Keep in mind also that you cannot meet all your children's needs. If possible, have them spend some time with other caring adults, persons whose beliefs about grief and death are similar to yours. This gives you breathing time to work on your own grief.

Dear God, I do want to think of my children, but I am so loaded down with my own grief. Give me wisdom and strength to help them, as I help myself. . . . Amen.

SCRIPTURE PASSAGES FOR REFLECTION

DEUTERONOMY 6:5-7

MARK 10:13-16

Share This Loss With Your Grown Children

Your older children are grieving too, and trying to understand how they will go on. What was your loved one's role in the family? Your role? How has the death of your loved one altered these roles? Be understanding of yourself and your children as all of you attempt to function and heal within this changed structure.

Communication is most important. Share your feelings with your children. When they ask you how you are, refrain from the automatic "I'm just fine." Let them know that you are struggling with your sorrow. Be open to hearing their thoughts and feelings.

Let your loss draw you closer. Look at pictures and talk about family experiences. Cry together. Encourage sharing regrets. Remember the fun times and laugh together. Use informal times to do this, as well as scheduled life celebration occasions.

Be specific as to what your children can do for you. They want to help, but may not know what to do, or they may stifle you with too much advice and caring. Indicate what you need, when, and how. You might even estimate how long you want certain kinds of assistance. And don't forget to show appreciation, being very specific.

You may need to set limits on what you will do for your children. They may think, now that you are "free" and "need something to do," that you have unlimited time and energy. When you are asked, state what you are willing to do. It is your life; be responsible for it. Be firm. Also, don't let your children rush or push you into something you are not ready to do.

Most of all, reach out to them with love. Understand and accept their pain. Help them to see and touch yours. Embrace them, both physically and in your thoughts.

Dear God, Thank you for the gift of my grown children. Help me to see their special abilities and needs. And help us to relate to each other in caring ways. . . . Amen.

SCRIPTURE PASSAGES FOR REFLECTION

PROVERBS 3:1-6

EPHESIANS 3:14-19

Welcome the Unexpected

There's really no way to avoid any surprises, is there? They just happen, those little things that devastate you and push the "tears" button. Take a moment to remember some of those things that have triggered those times of instant grief for you, and let the tears flow again.

As I think back, I remember some incidents that brought tears for me: hearing the old song "Welcome to My World," seeing my loved one's neatly printed tabs on file folders, finding the Christmas card he lost and never gave to me, having to write "Deceased" on a letter to be returned, looking through a box of recipes and seeing his favorite ones.

The temptation is to avoid these triggers, but they can actually help you to slowly let go of the pain you are carrying. Welcome these small reminders, especially if you are alone. Let the tears flow; they bring healing. They let you focus on specifics about which to grieve. If you are in a public place when these incidents occur, you may feel more comfortable in a restroom or quiet corner. But don't feel that you have to hide. Your tears are natural and normal. And don't murmur, "I'm sorry" if you are with friends. When you are finished crying, simply say, "Thanks for being here with me."

Be thankful that you can grieve and express your feelings. Nothing is more stifling than always holding in the pain. Expression of grief is necessary. Grieving hurts, but grieving also heals.

Dear God, You are the only one who is constant and nonchanging in my world. When the unexpected triggers my grief, hold me and let me cry. . . . Amen.

SCRIPTURE PASSAGES FOR REFLECTION

NUMBERS 23:19

HEBREWS 1:10-12

Venture Out Alone

Hand in hand. Two by two. It felt so right to be a pair. How can you turn the "we" pronoun to "I" and venture out alone? My first attempt to eat alone was on my birthday. I had planned a special day for myself, including lunch. But when the hostess asked, "Table for two?" I could only shake my head while tears filled my eyes. I stumbled behind her to the table that would be mine—alone. I read during the entire meal, with my book propped on a turned-over cup. Somehow I managed to eat. It wasn't easy, that first meal out alone, but I survived. The next time was easier.

Of course, it's also wise to exercise discretion. When social invitations come, imagine how you might feel in that situation before you accept. I did not do this when invited by friends to a dinner, with program following. They mentioned that another couple I knew would be joining us. As if being the fifth wheel wasn't enough, the tenor soloist sang love songs! Wrong choice.

Make it easier on yourself by choosing places and things to do in the beginning that were not favorites of you and your loved one. Otherwise, you will spend your time fighting memories. Also have an escape route in mind, just in case you need it.

Coming home alone can be even harder than going out alone. Turn on the radio or TV before you leave, so you will be greeted by voices or music when you open the door. Have something planned to do as soon as you get home: a call to a friend, a treat to eat, something you want to read, a specific TV program to watch, or a project to continue. If it will be dark before you return, always have a light turned on to welcome you.

To hear that "it will get easier" may be small comfort now, but someday that truth will be real.

Dear God, How can I possibly manage to go out alone? Give me courage and strength to take these first steps without my loved one by my side. . . . Amen.

SCRIPTURE PASSAGES FOR REFLECTION

PSALM 27:13, 14

HEBREWS 13:6

Employ the Wisdom of a "Worry Box"

When I begin to feel worried, I am always reminded of an unusual object I own: a tiny box from Guatemala with even tinier dolls inside. It is known as a "worry box." The one who uses it is invited to tell each of their worries to a different doll, place the dolls in the box, and put the lid on tightly. When they meet again, he or she checks in with each doll as to the assigned worry, which in many cases has gone away. What my worry box teaches me is that worries are usually not based on facts, but on what we fear may happen. Often, our fears never materialize at all.

How could you employ the wisdom of the worry box? Whenever possible, catch a worry in its first few moments. Confront it with a rational or positive thought. Ask yourself what is really true. If you don't have the facts to answer, then plan how and when you will get them. For example, if you begin to worry about paying your bills, take the time to list specifically what you owe and then calculate available funds.

If worries take hold before you realize it, try escaping by doing something physical. Take ten slow, deep breaths. Go for a walk. Mow the lawn. Or you might create a beautiful vacation spot and go there in your mind.

If you don't have a "worry buddy," it is well worth finding one. This is a person you can call at any time, someone who can objectively help you put your current worry into perspective. Sometimes just talking about it will drive the worry away.

If worry still persists, sit down for an "okay, worry, let's have it" session. Worry as hard as you can, and then, when you are worried out, grab your notebook, ask yourself what you can do about the situation, and make work notes. Then take any leftover worry, about which you can do nothing, and place it in the worry box. Put the lid on and forget it!

Dear God, You have invited me to cast my cares on you. Forgive me for trying to carry them all alone. I bring to you now what I can't manage. . . . Amen.

SCRIPTURE PASSAGES FOR REFLECTION

PSALM 46:1-7

MATTHEW 6:25-34

Improve Lonely and Alone Times

"What hurts the most?" my friends would sometimes ask me as I made my way through my journey of grief. My answer was always the same: "loneliness for my loved one." Death left a hole that no one else could fill. I felt cut off from my loved one, abandoned. The turning point for me was when I quit fighting loneliness, when I began to understand and embrace it. Loneliness is the acknowledgment that our loved one is gone, and facing reality is a necessary step in our grief journey.

But what does it mean, you may be wondering, *to embrace my loneliness?*

Spend time recalling both the good times and the not-so-good times with your loved one. What first attracted the two of you to each other? What qualities did you discover later? What were the favorite sharing times in your day? Your favorite foods and places to eat? What did you enjoy doing together? Look over the mementos you have saved. Choose the memories you want to keep and write about them in your journal.

Tears may come; you do not need to fight them. Welcome them and let them help you heal. Later you will be ready to reach out to others, not as a replacement or substitute, but because you need people in your life.

It is also important to realize that *aloneness* is not necessarily *loneliness*. Aloneness can be an opportunity to get to know yourself: your positive qualities and your feelings.

As you experience aloneness, spend time talking with God and becoming more comfortable in that relationship. Listen for God's voice. Find things to do alone that are fulfilling: reading, painting, gardening, writing, walking, listening to music, communing with nature. Gradually, you may even come to enjoy your alone time.

Dear God, No one except you knows how much I miss my loved one. The loneliness never goes away. Help me to feel you with me, as close as breathing. . . . Amen.

SCRIPTURE PASSAGES FOR REFLECTION

ISAIAH 41:10

PHILIPPIANS 4:8, 9

Focus Your Grief

Sometimes, we are tempted to try to fight off our grief, but we must remember: grief must be felt before it can be let go. I would like to suggest to you a four-step process that you may find helpful: (1) focusing: centering your attention, (2) visualizing: allowing memories and images to come to mind, (3) feeling: letting the feelings come, and (4) letting go: imagining yourself gently letting these feelings float away. I encourage you to move through these steps until they become comfortable, using the following statements.

Remember: focus ❧ visualize ❧ feel ❧ let go

❧ I now grieve the loss of future hopes, plans, and dreams with my loved one.

❧ I now grieve the loss of sharing everyday happenings with my loved one.

❧ I now grieve the loss of actually touching and being touched by my loved one.

❧ I now grieve the loss of our personal and private little stories and jokes.

❧ I now grieve the loss of our belonging together and functioning as a pair.

❧ I now grieve the loss of my loved one's continuing life experiences.

Continue by stating to yourself the losses that you feel most deeply and then moving through these four steps.

This is an exercise that you may want to repeat again and again as you feel losses in the future. Taking time to mourn each loss as it comes is difficult, but it will actually bring healing and release.

Dear God, I know I need to mourn my losses, but it hurts so! Accept my grieving heart and help me feel your healing touch, as I continue to grieve. . . . Amen.

SCRIPTURE PASSAGES FOR REFLECTION

ISAIAH 40:1-4

JOHN 14:1-7

Relive
That Day

There is one day you will always remember—the day your loved one died. Even tiny details are imprinted on your mind. How did that day begin for you? I remember standing at the window in the hospital room and thinking angrily, "How dare the sun rise on a beautiful day when my loved one is dying!"

Where were you when your loved one breathed the last? If you were present, what were you doing? Recall the scene and feel again what it was like. Who else was present? What did they do and say? What happened next? How did you manage to get through the rest of the day? Go through all of this in your mind, while letting yourself feel again.

Perhaps the news of your loved one's death was given to you by someone else. Who was this person and how was the message given? What was your response? Did you deny what you were told or accept it? What took place the rest of the day? Let the memories flow over you one more time. Close your eyes and do that now. When you have gone through the day and experienced the feelings, consciously let all of it go, and relax.

Yes, that was a terrible day, but you got through it. You survived. That first day of your personal journey through grief is over. You never have to go through that experience again. Neither do you have to remain locked in that day. You can go on.

Dear God, Thank you for being there on that awful day. Maybe I did not call on you or feel your presence as much as I could have; but you were there, loving me and encircling me with your everlasting arms. Be with me now, as I let those memories go. . . . Amen.

SCRIPTURE PASSAGES FOR REFLECTION

ISAIAH 40:28-31

MATTHEW 11:28-30

Write a Letter

Did you have time to say good-bye to your loved one? Even if you did, are there things you wish you had said? One very helpful way to deal with the things "left unsaid" is to write a letter to your loved one.

Write what you appreciate about your loved one. What will you remember? How was your life made better by your loved one being part of it? Pour out your longings and your love. Then read the letter aloud and put it in a safe place.

Continue to write additional letters whenever the mood strikes. The letters can be as long or short as you wish. Some may be angry ones—"Why did you leave me with. . . ." Some may focus on sorting out problems with your loved one "listening." My very first letter to my loved one was written in desperation. I had remembered something he had asked me to do for him in the hospital which I had not done. It bothered me for days. I grabbed a pad and started to write, page after page. The words poured out. Then I found myself writing as if he were answering me with his forgiveness. What comfort that brought!

My letters go into a large manila envelope, with special instructions for disposal printed on the outside.

Sometimes I re-read what I have written, finding release and relief, and trusting that my loved one understands.

On one celebration day, I wrote a special message. I had purchased a helium-filled balloon, to which I secured the note. I expected to have plenty of time to watch my important message waft its way. To my surprise, the balloon shot skyward and was soon out of sight. Was that symbolic of how fast my messages reach him?

Dear God, You know the longings of my heart. You know how much I miss my loved one. I trust that my loved one knows these things too. . . . Amen.

SCRIPTURE PASSAGES FOR REFLECTION

PSALM 36:7-10

2 CORINTHIANS 3:1-6

End
the Play

Was it by chance that you and your loved one met? Take time to recall that day. What led up to your meeting? Describe the events, as if it were a play, evolving around two central characters, you and your loved one. In your imagination, let the "play" unfold.

Now gather your life together into three acts. Start with Act One, the beginning years. Let scenes come to mind. See them, one by one, as they drift by. Dream the dreams. Experience again the joys of discovery and building, the two of you together.

What happened in the middle act of your life together, after your relationship was established? What was important then? This part of the play may have covered many years, many events. Relive those years. Take your time. Recall the pleasant, also the difficult. What do you choose to remember and treasure from this second act?

Now, play the final scene. How did it begin? Maybe you did not know in the beginning that it was the end. Now each tiny segment is etched in your mind's eye! Who were the other characters that joined you and your loved one? What preceded the final curtain? Sit quietly while the play comes to its end.

How would you change the closing scene, given the real-life situation as it was?

As you dwell on these scenes, allow yourself to respond as you would to any play that you saw, enjoying the happy and fun-filled moments and feeling the ache of sad scenes. You may even decide, even through the tears, that you have just witnessed a wonderful production.

Dear God, It is so hard to end the final scene. Help me just now. I pick my loved one up in my arms, holding him or her out to you. Receive my loved one into your love and care. . . . Amen.

SCRIPTURE PASSAGES FOR REFLECTION

PSALM 34:17-19

JOHN 3:11-16

Picture the Person
and
Feel the Spirit

Take a moment to describe your loved one. What were the color of his or her eyes and hair? What about facial features? Shape of hands and feet? Body structure and the way your loved one moved?

My husband was quite tall and thin, with china-blue eyes, sandy hair, long fingers and feet. He moved in a somewhat jerky manner. If only I could reach out and touch my loved one again! I would smooth back the few hairs falling forward on his forehead, touch the scar on his face, and pull his arms around me. . . . Tell me what you would do if you could actually see and touch your loved one once more.

Pause for a ritual, all your own. Visualize each part of your loved one's physical body. See it. Think of what you appreciated about it. Maybe one memory would be the mouth—the way it curved when your loved one smiled. Picture that smile, and say good-bye. Do this for each part of your loved one's body that you remember and love. When finished, lovingly offer your loved one's body to the spiritual realm, with your own service of dedication. Let your loved one's body go to be with God. Life and spirit still exist. We do not know in what form, nor do we need to know, in order to feel the presence of our loved one. Whatever was beautiful about your loved one and your relationship can stay with you. Listen for your loved one's words of comfort and advice. Respond with your messages. . . . Rejoice! The spirit lives on!

Dear God, Help me accept that my loved one's spirit is with you, and has become one with your Spirit. As I feel your presence now, I feel my loved one's presence too. . . . Amen.

SCRIPTURE PASSAGES FOR REFLECTION

PSALM 16:11

1 CORINTHIANS 15:44-49

Maintain Inner Communication

The day-to-day physical relationship with your loved one is no more, and you are mourning that loss. But you can continue a personal and inner relationship with your loved one.

Perhaps your loved one was quite vocal with words of advice. Mine did not tell me what he thought I should do, but somehow I sensed what his wise counsel would be. When we are perplexed, frustrated, and undecided, we can ask ourselves what our loved one's advice would be. We can "listen" carefully with a silent thank-you for what comes to mind. But it is important that we only accept and do what feels right to us, what we choose.

What did your loved one teach you? My loved one taught me especially about patience and acceptance of others. This would be a good time for you to start a page in your notebook, "What I appreciated about my loved one." List as many positive qualities as you can. Add more later as you think of them. From this list, choose what you would like more of in your life. Each of these deserves a page, one that might begin with, "I choose to be more patient by. . . ." List specific ways you could accomplish this. It is your choice to be more like your loved one, emulating qualities that you admire.

With friends, you talk about your day and share joys and sorrows. In your mind you can do this with your loved one. You probably know what some of your loved one's responses would be. These "conversations" can be meaningful, but should be brief, much like an "I'm-checking-in-with-you" time. Then get on with the living of your life.

Dear God, I am struggling with my new life alone, and it is so difficult. Help me to build on positives from my loved one's life. . . . Amen.

SCRIPTURE PASSAGES FOR REFLECTION

PSALM 19:7-14

2 TIMOTHY 3:12-17

Live in the Present

To live in memory, however tempting, is not to live at all. To live in the future, thinking it will be better, is also not to live. Today is the only day you have. How will you use it? The choices are yours. There are many possibilities from which to choose.

* How can you get your day off to a good start? (Some things that are healthy for your body? Some that are healthy for your soul?)

* What grief work needs to be done today? (Check for feelings of fear, regret, guilt, disappointment, anger, pain, loneliness, forgiveness, hope. Express these and other feelings aloud, on paper, or with a friend.)

* What ritual might you establish? (Find a special candle and place it beside a comfortable chair. Light it once a day and remember, for a little while, the light of your loved one in your life.)

* Look around until you have found something beautiful. Stay with it for a minute or two in appreciation. (Perhaps you will see sunlight patterns on a rug; a child's spontaneous smile; a mountain of apples in the grocery store; a bud ready to burst into bloom; the pure whiteness of milk in a colored glass; or multicolored designs on a tabby cat.)

* What can you do to make your home more livable? (Maybe you could swing the TV so it directly faces

your chair, put a stronger watt bulb in your reading light, organize one area in your clothes closet, or put a soft rug where you get out of bed.)

🌢 Be sure to do something for someone else today. (Someone would appreciate a smile when their day is blue, a cheerful call when they are not expecting it, or a note just to say "I love you.")

Before this day is over, stop to count your blessings. Today is yours. Live in it!

Dear God, I thank you for life. Each day is precious. Guide me in planning my day. I want to help myself where I can, and I want to help others in your name. . . . Amen.

SCRIPTURE PASSAGES FOR REFLECTION

PSALM 19:1-6

ROMANS 14:5-9

Acknowledge
the Imperfections

My marriage wasn't perfect; neither was yours. My loved one wasn't perfect either. No one is. Wanting perfect memories, we may elevate our loved one and our life together. Have you ever listened to someone rave about their loved one who died, and you didn't recognize the person they were describing? Looking at imperfections in our loved one may cause us to feel guilty. Accepting reality, however, is both healthy and helpful. Our loved one was real, warts and all. Our marriage was made on earth, not in heaven.

Are you making your loved one and your marriage larger than life? Allow yourself some quiet time to thoughtfully answer these questions. Be as honest as you can be.

* In what ways have I glorified my loved one?

* What behaviors of my loved one irritated me?

* What do I wish my loved one had said?

* How do I wish my loved one had been different?

* What parts of my marriage would I like to erase?

Sometimes the truth hurts. To truly grieve, however, is to grieve reality. We cannot grieve and let go if what we grieve is not real. To any degree that you can accept reality, be thankful. You have taken a step forward. Accept the imperfections of yourself, your loved one, and your marriage. Do this with love and understanding. . . . Now let go of the less-than-real. You no longer need to glorify in any way.

Dear God, You know my heart. You know my mind. You know I am not perfect. Neither was my loved one. Accept us both, with your understanding and forgiving love. . . . Amen.

SCRIPTURE PASSAGES FOR REFLECTION

PSALM 51:10-12

1 JOHN 1:6-10

Attend to
Unresolved Grief

What were the significant losses in your life prior to the loss of your loved one? Remember that these losses can be other than the death of someone you love. You may, for example, have lost a marriage, job, home, or treasured object. Begin with your childhood and move up through the present. List these losses in your journal notebook, leaving space after each loss. Then take time to consider for each what unresolved issues or feelings may remain.

Your present loss may activate feelings of grief and loss from the past. Are there emotions that still claim you? These feelings may attach themselves to your present grief, making separation and resolution difficult. If you have not fully mourned any of these losses from the past, do that now. Freeing yourself from past grief will enable you truly to grieve the loss of your loved one in the present.

Schedule a block of time to deal with each loss. For example, take the death of a parent. Sit quietly and let that parent come to mind. Visualize your interactions. What do you remember with deep emotion? Let the feelings come, relive them, and then let them go. What would you like to say to your parent? Say it now, anything. You can't hurt them.

Let it all out, the good and the bad. Then tell your parent good-bye. Re-image your parent and your new relationship. You may choose to do all of this by writing a letter, then destroying the letter. Deal with each loss on your list, in the way that works best for you, and feel the release of resolved grief.

Dear God, In the midst of my present loss, I did not recognize my leftover grief. Help me to finish my grieving from the past, and then to let it go. Accept all my grief and grant me your peace. . . . Amen.

SCRIPTURE PASSAGES FOR REFLECTION

PSALM 25:4-7

PHILIPPIANS 3:13-16

Forgive and Find Peace

Some surprising things can surface in the wake of a great loss. Shortly after my loved one's death, a member of his family began an extended personal attack against me. In return, my accumulated frustrations and anger became focused on this person, leaving little emotional energy to deal with my grief. Fortunately, I was able to stop and spend time considering why the person was behaving in this manner. In the end, I was able to understand, accept, and then to forgive.

Perhaps you have heard someone say, "Well, I'll forgive, but I'll never forget." There is a resentment just beneath those words that may leave you wondering whether he or she has really forgiven at all. Honest forgiveness brings closure and a sense of peace. Anger, bitterness, and resentment held inside keeps us restless, and we are not free to get on with the grief work we need to do.

In the early days of our grief we may angrily lash out at others—God, doctors and hospital staff, even the one who has died. Someone must be to blame for what happened! Perhaps we turn reproachfully upon ourselves, and guilt and anger may follow. We need an understanding person to hear and accept these feelings.

Schedule some time for soul-searching. Think about who or what you resent. Consider your loved one. Take each individual or event in turn and stay there until you come to some understanding of the "why." If a person is involved and forgiveness for what they have done is needed, actually say the person's name and "I forgive you for. . . ."

Forgiveness of self is perhaps the most difficult. Start with understanding your behavior. "Why did I do what I did?" Consider, with love. Then say to yourself, "I forgive you for. . . ." You may want to say to your loved one, "I'm sorry that I. . . ." Receive your loved one's words of forgiveness.

Dear God, You have forgiven me. Can I do less than forgive others? Sometimes it is difficult to do this, and I need your help. . . . Amen.

SCRIPTURE PASSAGES FOR REFLECTION

PSALM 130

MATTHEW 6:9-15

Let Nature Heal

Step with me into the world of nature, in reality or through imagery. Experience the sense of belonging, harmony, and peace that can be found there, and make these impressions part of you. If you're not sure where to begin, consider the following suggestions.

* Walk in a gentle rain. Get in step with the pattern of the raindrops. Smell the earth's reception. Tilt your head back and feel drops on your face—cleansing, healing. Avoid the puddles, or choose to walk through them—defiantly. Search for a rainbow when the sun interrupts the rain. Claim its promise.

* Keep vigil until you see the first snowflake. Watch it being joined by a host of others. Stay with the scene until the drab winter world becomes white and pure. Everything is sculptured with softened lines! Absorb the stillness. Feel total peace.

* The sky is yours for watching. Experience a sunrise and sunset in the same day. And, in between, watch blue skies, gray skies, and angry skies—something to match all your moods. Take an hour or two to dream along with the billowy clouds. Float with the scenes you imagine. Let the clouds take you wherever you want to go.

* Find a flower and trace each petal with gentle fingers. Smell its fragrance. This flower is different

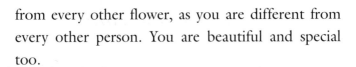

from every other flower, as you are different from every other person. You are beautiful and special too.

🌿 Find the strongest tree and put your arms around it. It is immovable! You can't see its roots, but you know they are there, reaching deep into the earth. In winter the tree looks dead, but you know it is alive.

🌿 Travel with the tiny twig being carried by a rushing stream. Feel the wind hitting head-on; turn, and let it push you home.

Dear God, Open my eyes! Help me to connect with the rhythms and cycles in the world you have created, and in so doing, connect and be at peace with you. . . . Amen.

SCRIPTURE PASSAGES FOR REFLECTION

PSALM 104:1-23

1 CORINTHIANS 15:40-41

Resolve the Guilt

Are you bound up with guilty feelings? Oh, you say, as I did, "I don't have any regrets," only to realize later that you have hidden certain feelings of guilt.

Find your Journal notebook. At the top of a page, write "I Feel Guilty About." Without hesitation, list any guilt or regret that comes to mind. Give yourself plenty of time, and get them all out. Don't stop to rationalize.

Now go back and look objectively at these entries, one by one. As you look at them carefully, you may come to see that some of them are not truly your fault. Honest mistakes or failings are not something we can control. As you look at your list, though, you may realize that there are some points for which you must accept blame. If so, spend some time in repentance. Allow yourself to feel your regret.

Then go forward to resolve your guilt. You may need to ask forgiveness from the person you have wronged—even if it is asking forgiveness from your loved one in the quietness of your own heart. Ask God to forgive. Take advantage of the resources your church offers. The Catholic Church, for example, offers the sacrament of reconciliation as a powerful tool in coming to know God's forgiveness. Finally, forgive yourself, even if you are only able to do that a little at a time.

Guilty feelings may come again. Take the time to consider whether they are legitimate feelings of guilt and then do what you need to do to resolve them. If guilt still remains despite all your work, get assistance. Your priest, pastor, or rabbi is standing by to listen and help. Professional counselors and understanding friends may be available as well. Unresolved guilt will hold you back in your journey through grief and can even cause physical ailments. Resolve it now.

Dear God, You are always there, ready to forgive. Help me to feel your forgiveness. But it is not enough to say "I'm sorry." Help me to hurt others less, and to help more, as you have taught me. . . . Amen.

SCRIPTURE PASSAGES FOR REFLECTION

PSALM 32:1-5

1 TIMOTHY 1:12-17

Face
Your Fears

Losing a loved one may leave us overwhelmed by fears of many kinds. It is important to try to distinguish among various kinds of fear. Some of our fears are helpful, cautionary fears. On a busy street corner we are afraid of being hit by a vehicle, so we stop and look before we cross. Being afraid of dependency on sleeping medications, we limit their usage to a week or two.

There are other kinds of fears, however, that may entrench themselves and keep us from functioning well. Left unchallenged, a fear may multiply or go even deeper. We need to take control of any fear before it takes control of us. Of what are you afraid, really afraid, to the point that the fear stays with you much of the time? Take this fear and ask yourself the following questions:

* Is what I am afraid of happening now?

* Is it likely to happen tomorrow? Next week? Next month?

* What can I do to keep it from happening?

Take your answers to the last question and develop a plan for dealing with your fear. Be specific. For example, make notes to deal with the fear that you have cancer, as perhaps your loved one did. A plan might include listing all your physical symptoms, making an appointment with your doctor, and sharing your fears.

Once your plans are made you are able to look your fear in the face. Say, "I know you are here. I see you for what you are—only something that might happen sometime. I have devised a plan to deal with you, so you can let go of your hold on me."

Dear God, Sometimes fears sneak in and get hold of me. Help me to see past these fears to what I can do. When I have done my part, I turn the rest over to you. . . . Amen.

SCRIPTURE PASSAGES FOR REFLECTION

PSALM 91:1-7

JOHN 14:27

Express Your Anger

The children who come to my play therapy room have a very basic framework for behavior: "You can do anything you want except (1) hurt me, (2) hurt yourself, or (3) hurt the property." As simple as it is, this is probably helpful advice for grown-ups as well. When you express your anger, do not say or do anything to hurt another person. Do not turn your anger toward yourself, and do not hurt valuable property.

Most persons who have lost a loved one have some anger, ranging from mild to raging. Anger is a natural response to our feeling abandoned, violated, taken advantage of, etc. Unfortunately, many of us have been taught that anger is bad and should not be expressed. Anger does not go away by itself. It can smolder and be dumped on undeserving others. It can be suppressed and surface later, manifested in physical ailments, anxiety, or depression.

It is best to deal with the issue of anger honestly. Collect your angry feelings and find the release that works best for you. Always say what you are angry about, preferably aloud, as you release the anger. A friend of mine saves broken dishes and furniture in her garage to smash against the wall when she is angry. Hitting the bathtub with a rolled-up towel, digging in the garden, scrubbing the floor, smashing the ball in a tennis or golf game, and walking fast are other possibilities. For some, venting anger in physical ways may be counterproductive. Perhaps they could talk out their anger: alone, with a nonjudgmental person, or in a support group. Or writing may be their means of expression, even though they may choose to destroy these statements at a later time. The important thing is to continue to release your anger in acceptable ways.

Dear God, Sometimes I am angry at you too, but I know you can handle it! After my anger is spent, I am so drained! Hold me, soothe me, and help me heal. . . . Amen.

SCRIPTURE PASSAGES FOR REFLECTION

PSALM 103:8-13

EPHESIANS 4:29-32

Sort Through Your Loved One's Belongings

The day after the services for my loved one, I was pressed by circumstances to let most of his clothing go. I had no opportunity to choose certain garments to keep or to say good-bye to the rest. If I could do it again, I would do it differently. I encourage you to resist pressure that may be put upon you and to wait until you are ready to deal with your loved one's things.

The time will come when you can better focus your thoughts, when you aren't swept away with every reminder of your loved one. One day, you will find yourself wondering about someone who might be able to put one of your loved one's belongings to good use; then you will know it is time to begin.

The actual process may take a day or two, or you may spend months at this task. You might want someone you trust to help you. As you do your sorting, picture your loved one wearing the garments or using the objects. Take time to say to yourself or your friend, "I remember when my loved one. . . ." You might write some of these memories, and the feelings that surface, in your Journal notebook.

Choose carefully in deciding which objects to keep. You may, for example, have a special memory associated with an object. For a long time I carried my loved one's pocket comb in my purse. Each time I touched it, I remembered seeing him comb his hair, how he looked, and his smile. Think of people who would appreciate having things that belonged to your loved one. Distribute these with love. Gather the rest together and find charities where they will be welcomed.

Your final task is to select a drawer, a chest, a box, or a shelf where you can contain the possessions of your loved one that you choose to keep. There will be times in the days ahead when you will want to visit these objects. Hold them, one by one, think of your loved one, and treasure the memories.

Dear God, Taking care of all these things that belonged to my loved one is so difficult. You understand and accept the ache in my heart as I do this. . . . Amen.

SCRIPTURE PASSAGES FOR REFLECTION

ISAIAH 54:10

JOHN 14:15-21

Recognize the Special Challenges Men Face

"Act like a man," the message fed to most males, translates to "Be strong, don't show your feelings, and never cry." Boys are programmed to squelch their tears, while little girls are handed tissue! By adulthood, men have built a wall around themselves and their feelings, while women have built a bridge to others. Thus, women may have a support group already in place for sharing their feelings when sorrow comes. Men, on the other hand, have buddies, not confidants. The time they spend with other men is usually work- or sports-oriented. A man's closest friend and confidant may have been his wife. Now she is gone and his compass in life is missing. The temptation to remarry is therefore often greater for a man, and other people may encourage this. But it is crucial that a man take time to deal with his grief first.

Part of this process is being patient. Men are problem-oriented and may see grief as something to be fixed, like taking an ailing car to a mechanic. Grief, however, is not as easy or predictable as a broken radiator!

It can be a great help to a recently bereaved man to have the friendship of another widower. They could meet for breakfast and talk things over. They might plan something to do together—golf, fishing, sports events, anything. They may, or may not, share their grief experiences, but just being with someone who understands will help. They might even join a support group, together.

Dear God, I know that my gender has nothing to do with the depth of grief I feel. Help me to express my sorrow to you and with others. May I feel understanding and compassion. . . . Amen.

SCRIPTURE PASSAGES FOR REFLECTION

PSALM 6:6-9

2 CORINTHIANS 1:3, 4

Find a
Support Group

"I don't like chocolate cake!" responded my young friend when I offered him a big piece. Then, a few minutes later, he confessed that he had never even tried chocolate cake! "I'm not a group-type person," you may be saying. If you haven't tried it, though, you don't know for sure!

The moment you step into a group of others dealing with grief, you feel the common denominator—all of you have lost someone dear. As you share and help each other, there forms an even deeper bond, drawing you even closer. You discover that your own "strange" actions are normal, not weird. The group can laugh as well as cry together, and it feels so good! Your feelings are understood and accepted. It is safe to be yourself. You find yourself looking forward to the next meeting. In between sessions you may talk with someone in the group or go out to eat together.

Where do you find a support group? Some local newspapers list all support groups. Or ask your doctor or religious leader. Community organizations and health centers are other referral possibilities. There may be a group for your age, at the time of day that you would like. If, after several sessions, you find that the group you have selected is not working for you, bow out. Another group may better meet your needs.

If a group is not available in your area, or the ones you tried were not suitable, consider starting one. It could be as simple as having a small group of widowed persons meet at a designated place, at a given time, on a regular basis. Or it could be more structured, and you could obtain help from a community group to organize and train leaders. Join the multitude of widowed persons who find group support beneficial.

Dear God, Use me as a support to others who are grieving as I am. Let your love and compassion flow through me to them. . . . Amen.

SCRIPTURE PASSAGES FOR REFLECTION

ECCLESIASTES 3:1-4

ROMANS 12:1-16

Share the Grief of Others— But Don't Be Overwhelmed

"I feel worse than I did before I came today. I feel so sad for all the people in our group. I'm not sure I should come again." This was the unsettling phone message I received after the beginning session of a grief support group I had organized. Out of caring, this person had taken on everyone else's grief on top of hers, going out with a much heavier load. It was a double whammy! No wonder this group member felt worse when she left.

When you are deep in your grief, it is natural for you to identify with another who is grieving. Not only is your grief brought to the surface, but you may absorb some of their pain. I believe that it is possible, however, to acknowledge another person's grief without accepting it as one's own. Here is the "Listener's Creed" that I wrote for my groups.

❧ I am aware of your grief. (I hear you.)

❧ I understand that you are grieving. (I am there, too.)

❧ I accept your grief—for you. (It is real, but it is yours.)

❧ I allow you to feel your own grief. (It is special to you.)

❧ Thus I honor you and your grief.

These statements may help you to listen in a caring way to others who are grieving, without taking away their grief or adding it to yours. Some of the members in my grief support groups choose to memorize these statements and to use them silently when they are listening to another person's grief. You may want to do this too.

Dear God, My own grief is about all I can handle right now. But I do care about others. Help me to show my love for them, but not take on their grief. . . . Amen.

SCRIPTURE PASSAGES FOR REFLECTION

JOB 2:11-13

COLOSSIANS 3:12-16

Celebrate

a

Birthday

The day that was once a celebration has become one of the most painful days of the year: it's your loved one's birthday. No one else may remember, but you do.

What do we do on birthdays? We celebrate. Let's you and I celebrate your loved one's birthday today. Tell me what you appreciate about your loved one's life. Use your loved one's name and say, "I celebrate that you. . . ." It's okay to repeat, okay to cry. If "celebrate" doesn't seem quite the right word, try "I'm thankful for your . . ." and continue to name your loved one's attributes and accomplishments, large and small. Give yourself plenty of time. Here's a chance to say all those things you might not have said. Your loved one accepts and understands. You may also want to include all of this in a happy birthday letter to put away and read again next year.

Ready for the present? First, recall a gift you enjoyed giving on your loved one's birthday or a surprise you planned. Maybe it was something your loved one wanted. Or was it a present or experience you wanted your loved one to have? Today, you can give the gift

of your love. Tell your loved one of your love, in as many ways as you can, or in one sentence. It is a gift with no strings attached, no conditions. Say it again. "I love you." It is the present you can give every day. In your heart, your loved one lives on and so does your love.

Dear God, I am thankful for my loved one's life. I am thankful that we met and that we had time together. Join me in celebrating that life today. Take my love for my loved one, as I give it now. . . . Amen.

SCRIPTURE PASSAGES FOR REFLECTION

PSALM 100:4, 5

1 CORINTHIANS 13

Choose
to Fulfill

As you embark on the project of building a new, meaningful life for yourself, you may find it helpful to ask yourself the following question: "What positive things would my loved one want for me? To happen in my life? For me to feel and be?" Listen to the voice of your loved one. List these wishes in your notebook. If you write a general one, like "To be happy," follow that with specific ways in which your loved one would want you to be happy. Make as long a list as you can. Take your time.

Now take time to consider the list carefully. Which of these things are you already working toward? Are there others that you realize now that you would like to do for yourself?

Write "I choose to . . ." before each one that you accept as your own choice. Add how you might do this. An example might be, "I choose to 'Be kind to myself' by asking a friend to help me with medical forms, eating more fruits and vegetables, buying a present for myself on my birthday, beginning a reasonable exercise program, etc."

Consider the following question: What if your situation were reversed? If your loved one remained, what would you wish for him or her? Make your list and compare. This exercise may give you things to add to your loved one's list for you.

Finally, talk or write to your loved one about all of this. Listen to the reply.

Dear God, I know my loved one wants me to be happy and enjoy living. You want these things for me too. Help me to remember this and choose to live again. . . . Amen.

SCRIPTURE PASSAGES FOR REFLECTION

PSALM 16:7-11

MARK 8:34, 35

Create Memorials

What is a memorial? According to Webster, "a memorial is something that keeps remembrance alive." You have seen many grand, public memorials, but small, private memorials can be just as important. My loved one always looked for the first dogwood to bloom in the spring, so I chose to plant a pink one where I can see it from the kitchen window and remember him. He loved young children, so I paid for a needy child to go to summer camp, in his memory.

- If your loved one enjoyed plants and flowers, you might create a small memorial garden with his or her favorites.

- Perhaps you could find a work of art, in the type your loved one appreciated, to place in your home.

- Could friends and family record their memories of your loved one—on paper, or on cassette tape or video?

- Compose a poem.

- How about making a wall collage of pictures from your life together?

- Treasured objects belonging to your loved one might be put in a beautifully decorated "Memory Box."

- Did your loved one have a collection that could be donated to a library, museum, or school?

❧ Consider what is needed in your faith community: altar flowers, a stained-glass window, bibles, camp scholarships. Or perhaps there are needs in your larger community: park equipment, shade trees, library books. Offer to purchase what you choose, and dedicate that to your loved one's memory. Educational institutions welcome memorial scholarships.

We can also give of ourselves in memory of our loved one. My first Thanksgiving alone, I helped serve meals at the Salvation Army, my loved one's favorite charity. As I served, I said to myself, "I'm doing this in memory of you."

Dear God, I want so much for memories of my loved one to live on. Help me as I choose memorials that honor my loved one's memory. . . . Amen.

SCRIPTURE PASSAGES FOR REFLECTION

ISAIAH 55:10-13

1 JOHN 4:7-12

Begin to Play (Again)

Steal a flower. Yes, you heard me right. On your next walk, snitch a flower or find an interesting rock or wood formation to bring home. Buy the candy you loved best as a child. Gobble it down, or savor every bite—however you ate it as a child. Next time, don't walk; skip (do you remember how?) when no one is watching. I dare you!

There is a playful child inside each of us that we normally ignore or push down. This is especially true when we are grieving. But the child within can help us heal, providing moments of blessed escape from the dreariness of grief. Here are more suggestions:

* On the next clear night find a bright star and make a wish. Say, "Star light, star bright, first star I see tonight. I wish I may, I wish I might, have the wish I wish tonight." (And yes, make a wish!)

* Think of something you probably shouldn't do but would like to, something that won't hurt you or anyone else. Do it, and don't tell!

* Read the comics first in the newspaper. When one strikes you as funny, let a chuckle begin and some sound come out of your mouth. Go ahead!

* Spend time in a store looking at the toys and games you enjoyed as a child. Recall the fun. Before you leave, purchase something to take

home, to play with alone or with someone else. Why not borrow a child for an afternoon? We are never too old to play!

Spend some time thinking of other possibilities. Only you know what you would most love to do, what would be the best way for you to "play."

Dear God, Maybe your enjoyment is watching us enjoy life. As you know, having fun is very hard for me to do right now. You remember me as a playful child. Help me to remember too and begin to play again. . . . Amen.

SCRIPTURE PASSAGES FOR REFLECTION

PSALM 126

MATTHEW 18:2-5

Volunteer and
Help Others

Do you feel as if you are somehow lacking purpose and meaning? Are you longing to feel satisfaction and happiness again? If so, as soon as you are emotionally and physically able, volunteer to help in an area of need. By volunteering, you give of yourself to someone in want because you care, not for financial gain or public recognition. In this giving of self, you will experience happiness and healing, even in your time of grief.

What ages do you enjoy being with: babies, children, youth, adults, older persons? What do you like to do, and what are your capabilities? Match what you know about yourself with an area of need in your community.

Ask among your friends and within your faith community for places where you could be of help. Some social service organizations offer volunteer placement. The list of volunteer organizations is endless. Here are a few: Action (includes Foster Grandparents), Habitat for Humanity, Meals on Wheels, Public Education Association (tutorial work in schools), SCORE (Service Core of Retired Executives), Big Brother/Big Sister.

When the message gets out that you are beginning to volunteer, you may be swamped with pleas for help. Be careful not to overextend yourself. In the beginning choose one form of service and commit yourself to fewer hours than you think you can handle. You can always add more time later. If, after a reasonable length of time, you don't feel good about what you are doing, look for a situation in which you do. It is important to know that what you are doing, however small, is making some difference in the world.

Dear God, There is so much distress and need in the world. Guide me to the place where I can be of service, and help me to minister in your name. . . . Amen.

SCRIPTURE PASSAGES FOR REFLECTION

DEUTERONOMY 15:10, 11

MATTHEW 25:35-40

Enter the Internet

You may already have a computer, an Internet provider, and be proficient at finding your way through sites on the Internet. If so, you can simply use your favorite search engine to find an abundance of grief-related materials and discussion groups.

On the other hand, this may be foreign territory for you. The early period of grief is not the time to select your first computer, get it installed, and become familiar with its workings. Instead, find a friend or family member to be your helper, accessing grief-related web sites for you. Read what other widowed persons are sharing from their grief. Look at the wealth of material on how to handle grief. Get your "helper" to print articles that you can take with you and read later. This will be enough for now.

Later, you may enjoy the challenge of joining the computer age. Take your time. Become familiar with the basic computer components and terms. Beginning computer literacy classes are given at community colleges and adult education centers. Persons over fifty can join Senior Net, which offers centers around the country where seniors can get practical help with purchasing and learning to use computers. Take someone with you when you are ready to purchase your computer system. Mail-order catalogs offer good bargains, but here again, get someone knowledgeable to help you.

It will take time to get your system up and running and for someone to help you in doing this. Be prepared to rant and rage at your computer. It is part of the learning process! Use of your computer and the Internet will open up a whole new world for you. E-mail in itself is a marvel! Just think, with e-mail, you will be able to send a message in seconds to anyone who also is on the Internet and to hear from them just as soon!

Dear God, You have created us with minds that can discover and invent, and I praise you. Help me to use the marvel of computers to receive help with my grief. . . . Amen.

SCRIPTURE PASSAGES FOR REFLECTION

GENESIS 1:27-29

COLOSSIANS 1:15-17

Generate
Some Laughter

With all the sadness in your life, your laughing mechanism may need oiling! Laughter is healing and brings momentary relief to the damaged soul. It helps to balance painful times.

First, give yourself permission to laugh. Excluding joy and laughter will not bring your loved one back. The sadness in your face is not the measure of how much you loved. Accept that it is okay to laugh.

Begin by "borrowing" from the laughter of others. When someone laughs, try to capture a little of what they are feeling. Let yourself laugh or at least smile. Observe little children at play. Borrow some of their fun. Join with them if you can. As smiling begins to become a little more familiar again, consider the following possibilities.

- Rent a funny video of your favorite comedian. Enjoy it alone or invite your friends for a fun evening, complete with popcorn and soft drinks.

- Look for humor in life situations and make jokes. Surprise others with, "Wait till you hear the funny thing that. . . ." Jokes about yourself are fine, as long as they are not put-downs. Always be kind to yourself.

❧ Spend some time remembering specific fun-filled incidents with your loved one. I could tell you about the time my loved one and I were sightseeing in a big city and a pigeon "let loose" right on my face! He laughed, but I didn't, until much later. Re-live your funny experiences and enjoy again. Bring more laughter into your life and congratulate yourself!

Dear God, Give me joy and gladness, in place of grief. Put a song of praise in my heart, instead of sorrow. . . . Amen.

SCRIPTURE PASSAGES FOR REFLECTION

ISAIAH 61:1-3

MATTHEW 5:1-10

Look in the Mirror

Your early sense of self was formed from reflections provided by parents and friends. Later, your loved one also provided reflections and your identity became closely intertwined with that other person. You became half of a whole.

As you work through the grief you are feeling, you may find it helpful to think more about the "reflections" you have seen.

First, think of yourself as a child and young person. Describe your personality. What were your strengths and weaknesses? How did you use your abilities and compensate for your weak areas? How did you approach problems? Name some accomplishments. Were you a leader or a follower? How did you feel about yourself?

Now let's move to the person you became after you were married. What parts of your personality became less apparent in relationship with your loved one? What traits did you develop in the context of your relationship?

Of course, the identity and roles filled by your loved one are no longer present. Also missing is the positive and negative feedback you received for being who you were. You are now faced with establishing a new identity, a new image in the mirror.

Ask someone who knows you well to enumerate your strengths and likable qualities. Rediscover the positive parts in you that were not used in your relationship with your loved one. Be aware of what you are now able to handle, and rejoice in your new areas of competence.

Look at the new person emerging in the mirror. Say to yourself, "I am not restricted by the past. I now think and act for myself. I am somebody. I am me, and I count. I can take as much time as I need to become the person that I choose to be."

Dear God, I believe that you have always seen me as special. But sometimes I have not seen myself that way. Help me to accept your image as true. . . . Amen.

SCRIPTURE PASSAGES FOR REFLECTION

PROVERBS 4:23-27

1 CORINTHIANS 13:11, 12

Consider Your Wedding Ring

It may be that the most powerful symbol of your marriage is the ring you have worn since you spoke your marriage vows. Now you have to decide what to do about this small object that means so much to you.

Consider the voices of those who continue to wear their rings:

🌿 "Wearing my ring tells the world that my heart is still with my loved one."

🌿 "My rings go with 'Mrs.,' which I continue to use."

🌿 "I wear my rings out of habit. I would feel naked without them."

🌿 "Taking off my ring would be another loss. I've had enough losses."

🌿 "My wedding rings provide protection."

Of course, there are also those who choose to stop wearing their rings:

🌿 "I am no longer married. My ring is a symbol of the marriage that ended."

🌿 "I am ready for a new life, and perhaps a new relationship."

🌿 "Taking off my rings does not mean I am looking for a new relationship. It simply means I am not married."

🌿 "My loved one was ill for so many years. I need to move on."

❧ "When I took off my ring I knew that I had finally faced the fact that my loved one had died."

❧ "I had my own ceremony when I took off my ring."

There are also many creative options for you to consider. Rings may be taken off and made into different forms of jewelry. Some are passed on to heirs. Others are worn on the other hand or on a chain around the neck. It is your personal choice to remove your rings or to continue to wear them. With either choice, you can always remember what your rings symbolized and the love you shared.

Dear God, As with other big decisions, I can take my time to consider taking off my wedding rings. I trust you to be with me through this and all decisions. . . . Amen.

SCRIPTURE PASSAGES FOR REFLECTION

GENESIS 2:18-24

ROMANS 7:1, 2

Proceed Slowly With Dating

Can you remember your very first date? Much has happened since then! Dating has changed; you have changed. Take your time in entering into the romantic world again. Check that your former relationship has been transformed from present reality to loving memory. Live with your new identity for a while; get to know this person you have become, apart from your loved one. Allow yourself to begin to feel comfortable with the many changes.

A much safer and easier way to begin is to make friends with those of the opposite sex just for the sake of friendship, built around mutual interests and activities. This gives you the chance to get to know new people and become more comfortable with them. Later, you may choose to assess these friendships and look for dating possibilities.

How do you find these persons with whom to build friendships? Tell your friends what you are looking for. If you have always wanted to try your luck at acting, "throwing" a pot, wood carving, or car maintenance, there are classes for these ventures and endless others. Join clubs like Toastmasters or Sierra (hiking). Look within your faith community. If you like to entertain, invite singles as well as couples to your home.

Dating still carries with it selection and seriousness. Before beginning to date a specific person, you need to be up-front with that person, discussing what each of you wants and expects. In the beginning, meeting for lunch and an activity might be easier than candle-light dinners. Be certain within yourself as to your physical and sexual boundaries. It is very difficult to back up while in a relationship. Proceed slowly. Save spaces in your life for your other friends, including those of the opposite sex. Allow a long period of dating, plus some non-dating real-world experiences before considering remarriage.

Dear God, You created man and woman to be together. Be with me in a special way as I make new friendships. May they be wholesome and fulfilling. . . . Amen.

SCRIPTURE PASSAGES FOR REFLECTION

PROVERBS 27:10

JOHN 13:34

Contemplate Remarriage

Did you and your loved one ever have a conversation in which you asked one another, "If anything happened to me, would you remarry?" What were your answers? My loved one and I both said the same thing, "I would want you to marry again, but I don't think that I will." What your loved one said may influence you, if you begin to think about this step. Negative comments, even in teasing, may haunt you. Positive ones may help free you to make your own decision.

Often friends (usually married ones!) try to play matchmaker for getting widowed persons married again. But a quick look around us dispels the myth that married people are always happier. Widowed persons can have a full and rewarding life without remarrying. It is important to realize that you are free to choose to marry again and also free to choose not to marry again. It is possible to find happiness inside marriage or outside.

There are a number of ingredients necessary for a successful marriage. Two people must (1) be reasonably healthy—physically, emotionally, mentally, and spiritually, (2) have shared interests and values, and (3) be able to communicate with each other. Using these criteria, how do you and the person you are considering for remarriage score? Remember to factor in any problems peculiar to your situation, including stepchildren, finances, and housing situations. Perhaps more then any other decision, this is one in which you must give yourself all the time you need to be realistic and to make a wise decision.

You are older, wiser, and more mature than the last time you contemplated marriage. Decide what is important, what you are not willing to do without. And don't forget than you can choose to create your own happiness alone and take care of yourself.

Dear God, This decision of remarriage is so important. I ask that you be part of it, leading and guiding me in the right direction. I ask your blessing. . . . Amen.

SCRIPTURE PASSAGES FOR REFLECTION

PSALM 119:105, 106

2 CORINTHIANS 6:14

Measure Growth and Accomplishments

Grief makes way for growth. You may not realize it, but you have probably already grown in positive ways since the death of your loved one. Often we cannot see our own personal growth until we look back, consider how we used to feel, and then measure the gain.

The exercise below may help you to see the progress you've made. As you consider each area, put a (1), (2), or (3) to indicate your progress, with (1) indicating a small amount of growth and (3) indicating a great deal of growth.

I have:

    ___ mourned what I have lost,

    ___ found persons with whom to share grief,

    ___ allowed myself to cry,

    ___ deepened my personal faith,

    ___ become more compassionate toward others,

    ___ handled my finances and personal affairs,

    ___ recalled memories of my loved one, without pain,

    ___ become aware of new strengths in myself,

    ___ taken care of my health,

    ___ found joy in simple pleasures,

___ felt glad to be alive,

___ survived anniversaries,

___ reached out to others in need,

___ begun to sleep longer and more soundly,

___ found fulfilling activities,

___ taken positive steps to cope with loneliness,

___ begun to smile and laugh again.

Look at each area again, and as you do, take time to consider fully (and give yourself credit for!) the personal growth you have experienced and the difficult tasks you have accomplished.

Dear God, In looking back, I do see where I have changed and grown. I acknowledge your central part in all of this and I thank you. . . . Amen.

SCRIPTURE PASSAGES FOR REFLECTION

PSALM 139:1-12

2 THESSALONIANS 2:16, 17

Take Stock
and Set Goals

It has been a long journey, this journey through grief. Survival may have been all that you could manage in the beginning. Gradually, though, you were able to confront your loss and express your grief. This may be a good time for you to stop and take a few moments to look back.

What has this journey of grief been like for you so far? Start at the beginning of your grief. What happened at important steps along the way? What were your feelings? What were you able to let go? Feel the release that took place. Where have you taken control? Be specific. What things do you feel good about?

Where are you now in your journey? What do you find is most important to you now? What do you value? Who are you, now that you are no longer half of a whole? Describe this person. Go over the strengths you have discovered, strengths that are now being used. What do you appreciate about the life you are living? Think of the relationships you have established and of previous ones you have deepened.

As long as there is life, there can be growth. What do you want to happen in your life in the next year? Find your Journal notebook. Finish the sentence, "To continue my journey through grief, I choose to. . . ." Write as many endings as you can. From these endings, try to establish at least three goals. Choose reasonable ones, preferably short-term. Put each goal on a separate page, with specific actions for reaching that goal. What might you do to help yourself achieve that goal? Include how you will measure progress.

As you work toward meeting your continuing goals, be firm with yourself. But also be understanding and forgiving when you fall short. You can always begin again.

Dear God, The journey has been long and hard. Thank you for being with me. There is still more to do. Please stay with me. . . . Amen.

SCRIPTURE PASSAGES FOR REFLECTION

PSALM 119:28-44

PHILIPPIANS 4:10-13

Seek Additional Help

You may find that you simply are not getting the help you need in your journey through grief. How would you know if this is true? Ask yourself if you have:

- unresolved conflicts from your relationship with your loved one that still haunt you,
- intense feelings of anger or guilt that you cannot express or resolve,
- loss of contact with the outside world, resulting in withdrawal,
- growing dependence on alcohol and/or other drugs,
- measurable sleeplessness for more than three months,
- loss of weight, indicated by clothes being two sizes too big, or comparable weight gain with clothes too small,
- inability to part with or move even one object that belonged to your loved one,
- absolutely no one with whom to share your grief.

If one or more of these is true for you, be kind to yourself and seek help. It is a sign of strength, not weakness, to do this. You can find referrals to a professional counselor through your church or your

doctor. Ask for someone trained in dealing with grief issues.

If you know you need to do this, don't hesitate. Do it now.

Dear God, I'm at the end of my rope and barely hanging on. Others can be your hands in the world. Help me to find the right person for me. Work through that person to help me. . . . Amen.

SCRIPTURE PASSAGES FOR REFLECTION

PSALM 91:14-16

2 CORINTHIANS 1:3-11

A note from the author

Dear grieving one,

Thank you for opening the door and inviting me into your world. It has been good to share from my grief and loss. In my imagination, I have listened to your sorrow and pain.

In one sense, I am not leaving you. You can return to these pages whenever you wish. Now, however, you need to move on: measure where you are, determine what needs to be done, and continue to grow. Check the resources list for additional help.

Although I do not even know your name, you were held in my heart during the many early hours while this book took shape. Be assured that I will continue to think of you and remember you with the following prayer.

Marta Felber

Dear God, I thank you for this special person, and for our connection in the pages of this book. Lay your hand of blessing on this grieving one's head; strengthen and guide forever more. . . . Amen.

SCRIPTURE PASSAGES FOR REFLECTION

NUMBERS 6:24-26

Resources

BOOKS

Inspirational

Getting Through the Night: Finding Your Way After the Loss of a Loved One, by Eugenia Price
A small book with a deep message that, through God's strength, we can one day learn to live again in the morning light.

The Journey Through Grief: Reflections on Healing, by Alan D. Wolfelt
This spiritual companion encourages mourners to think with the heart and the soul. It carries an affirming message of faith, hope, and healing.

Listening to Nature: How to Deepen Your Awareness of Nature, by Joseph Cornell
A beautiful book, with stunning photos, inspiring quotations from famous naturalists, and activities to deepen awareness of nature's beauty.

Meditations for the Widowed, edited by Judy Osgood
Thirty-three men and women offer what helped them turn hopelessness to hope, enabling them to heal and build new lives for themselves.

A Pilgrimage Through Grief, by James E. Miller
With lyrical prose and evocative photographs, James E. Miller provides a pilgrimage from grief to growth, from hurt to healing.

When Grief Breaks Your Heart, by James W. Moore
This book explores how our faith can help us in times of loss through the comfort and healing that come only from God.

Blessed Are Those Who Mourn: Comforting Catholics in Their Time of Grief, by Glenn M. Spencer, Jr.

The author, a chaplain and director of pastoral care, looks at the grieving process within the context of the church and the sacraments. Explains how to grow from the grief experiences.

The Courage To Grieve: Creative Living, Recovery, and Growth Through Grief, by Judy Tatelbaum

Deals with all aspects of grief and its resolution. Easy to read and very practical.

The Healing Journey Through Grief: Your Journal for Reflection and Recovery, by Phil Rich

This guide invokes the healing power of writing to provide you with a means for collecting your thoughts, sorting out your feelings, and taking an active part in your own recovery.

I Can't Stop Crying: It's So Hard When Someone You Love Dies, by Rev. John D. Martin and Frank D. Ferris

Deals with permission to grieve and suggests steps for rebuilding.

Living Through Mourning: Finding Comfort and Hope When a Loved One Has Died, by Harriet Sarnoff Schiff

With tenderness and wisdom, the author writes about the feelings of isolation, fear, anger, and loss that are common to friends and relatives when a loved one dies.

Living When a Loved One Has Died, by Earl A. Grollman

Gently, honestly, and with simple compassion, the author says what must be said to help confront death and go on living. Easy to read, but profound.

Mourning and Mitzvah: A Guided Journal for Walking the Mourner's Path Through Grief to Healing, by Anne Brener
Explores in depth the place where psychology and religious ritual intersect. Many useful activities. Also helpful to those outside the Jewish tradition.

On Death and Dying, by Elizabeth Kubler-Ross
Remains a classic. Dr. Kubler-Ross explores her now famous five stages of death: denial and isolation, anger, bargaining, depression, and acceptance. The book brings hope not only to the dying but to the loved ones who remain.

Seven Choices: Taking the Steps to New Life After Losing Someone You Love, by Elizabeth Harper Neeld
An inspiring and profoundly moving book that offers hope, comfort and advice to those who have suffered loss by moving the grieving person through seven phases.

To Begin Again: The Journey Toward Comfort, Strength, and Faith in Difficult Times, by Naomi Levy
The author tells us how to survive, emotionally and spiritually, when we feel overwhelmed by grief, loss, or life itself.

Understanding Grief, Helping Yourself Heal: A Compassionate Guide to Coping With the Death of Someone Loved, by Alan D. Wolfelt
This book provides a safe place for the bereaved to be in touch with their thoughts and feelings, and move toward healing the pain. Also presents guidelines for support groups.

When Bad Things Happen To Good People, by Harold S. Kushner
A classic self-help guide, by the respected rabbi, explains how to find comfort and strength in the face of tragedy and to understand God's role in recovery.

Loss of a Spouse

Grief Expressed: When a Mate Dies, by Marta Felber
> The author offers her actual grief work after the death of her husband. The reader is invited to do their own work by her side, on beautifully designed and comforting pages.

How to Survive the Loss of a Love, by Melba Colgrove, Harold H. Bloomfield, and Peter McWilliams
> A best-seller. Has ninety-four suggestions for surviving, healing, and growing.

I'm Grieving as Fast as I Can: How Young Widows and Widowers Can Cope and Heal, by Linda Feinberg
> Speaks to the unique needs and challenges of the young widowed.

Men and Grief: A Guide for Men Surviving the Death of a Loved One, by Carol Staudacher
> Provides an insightful and thought-provoking look at the problems faced by men in grief as they go through the most internally hurtful time of their lives.

On Your Own: A Widow's Passage to Emotional and Financial Well-Being, by Alexandra Armstrong and Mary R. Donahue
> The authors profile four composite women at ages 43, 50, 62, and 75 to examine different life situations and needs. Very practical help is given.

Swallowed by a Snake: The Gift of the Masculine Side of Healing, by Thomas R. Golden
> An excellent guide for understanding and undertaking the masculine path of healing.

When Your Spouse Dies, by Cathleen Curry
> Writing directly and sensitively about her own journey, the author helps others deal creatively with

theirs. She establishes eight practical guideposts for getting through the first year.

Widow to Widow: Thoughtful, Practical Ideas for Rebuilding Your Life: Challenges, Changes, Decision-Making and Relationships, by Genevieve Davis Ginsburg
Updated and revised, this book explores every aspect of the widow's world.

The Widow's Resource: How to Solve the Financial and Legal Problems That Occur Within the First Six to Nine Months of Your Husband's Death, by Julie A. Calligaro
In addition to the above help, this book contains sample letters and a "To-Do-List" on perforated pages that tear out for easy use.

Will I Ever Be Whole Again?: Surviving the Death of Someone You Love, by Sandra P. Aldrich
This sensitive book is written from the author's personal experience of the death of her husband. Her insight is comforting, her wisdom soothing, and her direction inspiring.

How to Comfort Children

Healing the Bereaved Child, by Alan D. Wolfelt
A comprehensive book describing how a grieving child thinks, feels, and mourns. Explains six needs of the mourning child and how to help, and much more.

How Do We Tell the Children?: A Step-by-Step Guide for Helping Children Two to Teen Cope When Someone Dies, by Dan Schaefer and Christine Lyons
Drawing on more than three decades of experience helping families in crisis, the author reveals what children already know, what they are capable of understanding, and how adults can help them cope with feelings of grief, fear, and loss.

Special Needs

Beyond the Relaxation Response, by Herbert Benson
This volume builds on the best-selling original *The Relaxation Response*, adding the Faith Factor to the meditative technique.

Celebrate Yourself: Making Life Work for You, by Dorothy Corkille Briggs
A practical step-by-step guide to building a positive self-image that will enhance every area of life and create new joy and satisfaction.

The Courage to Laugh: Humor, Hope and Healing in the Face of Death and Dying, by Allen Klein
Provides poignant wisdom and inspirational examples from a world in which we think there is no laughter. The author shows how to face the grieving process with dignity, compassion, and yes, even laughter.

The Good News About Worry, by William Backus
The author, a Christian psychologist, applies the truth of the gospel in very practical terms to problems of anxiety, fear, and worry.

Making Peace With Your Parents: The Key to Enriching Your Life and All Your Relationships, by Harold H. Bloomfield, with Leonard Felder
Whether or not your parents are alive, this book will help you come to terms with this fundamental relationship, and help you become more fulfilled in the process.

Meditation Made Easy, by Lorin Roche
A comprehensive book that helps you overcome meditation obstacles and gets you started with meditation that will become both natural and vital.

What Color Is Your Parachute?: A Practical Manual for Job-Hunters and Career-Changers, by Richard N. Bolles
This book is revised every year.

The Worrywart's Companion: Twenty-One Ways to Soothe Yourself and Worry Smart, by Dr. Beverly Potter
Brimming with practical ideas you can try today, this book includes twenty-one simple things you can do when you feel a worry coming on. The author believes that worry is a behavior that can be unlearned.

MAGAZINES

Bereavement:
A Magazine of Hope and Healing
Bereavement Publishing, Inc.
5125 N. Union Blvd., Suite 4
Colorado Springs, CO 80918
888-604-HOPE (4673)
www.bereavementmag.com
e-mail: grief@bereavement.com
Published six times a year. Stories, articles, and poems are written by readers who are bereaved themselves. Regular departments are presented by professionals in the field of grief intervention, addressing many issues.

In Accord
1941 Bishop Lane, Suite 202
Louisville, KY 40218
800-346-3087
www.hope2k.com
www.accord-grief.com
e-mail: accord123@aol.com
Published quarterly. Includes inspirational, educational, and practical articles designed to help the reader develop skills to cope with grief. It also provides additional services and resource information. It is a perfect gift that keeps on giving.

MAIL-ORDER SOURCES FOR BOOKS AND OTHER GRIEF MATERIALS

Accord
1941 Bishop Lane, Suite 202
Louisville, KY 40218
800-346-3087
www.hope2k.com

Bereavement Publishing, Inc.
5125 N. Union Blvd., Suite 4
Colorado Springs, CO 80918
888-604-HOPE (4673)
www.bereavementmag.com

Centering Corporation
1531 N. Saddle Creek Rd.
Omaha, NE 68104
402-553-1200
www.webhealing.com/centering

Compassion Books
477 Hannah Branch Rd.
Burnsville, NC 28714
828-675-5909
www.compassionbooks.com

Willowgreen
509 West Washington Blvd.
Fort Wayne, IN 46802
219-424-7916
www.willowgreen.com
jmiller@willowgreen.com

ORGANIZATIONS

AARP Grief and Loss Programs
601 E. Street N.W.
Washington, DC 20049
(202) 434-2260
www.aarp.org/grief and loss
e-mail: griefandloss@aarp.org
>   Offers a wide variety of bereavement programming
>   (e.g., one-to-one outreach, such as its Widowed
>   Person Service, support groups and educational
>   meetings) that serve bereaved persons and their
>   families.
>
>   AARP offers free, self-paced classes in using
>   computers and communicating through the Internet
>   at www.aarp.org/ei.
>
>   For free copy of "On Being Alone" and/or to
>   learn location of closest program to you, contact
>   AARP.

American Association of Pastoral Counselors
9504A Lee Highway
Fairfax, VA 22031-2303
(703) 385-6967
www.aapc.org
e-mail: info@aapc.org
>   A pastoral care referral service that provides a center
>   and counselor in caller's local area.

The American Psychiatric Association
1400 K. Street, NW
Washington, DC 20005
(202) 682-6000
www.psych.org
e-mail: apa@psych.org
>   When you call, ask for the telephone number of the
>   district branch of the American Psychiatric
>   Association for your state. Someone at the district

branch will then be able to give you the names of doctors in your local area.

The American Psychological Association
750 First St. NE
Washington, DC 20002
(202) 336-5500
www.apa.org
e-mail: public.affairs@apa.org
Contact for the telephone number of the executive officer of the association serving your state. That person will refer you to therapists in your local area.

Bereavement and Loss Center of New York
170 East 83rd Street
New York, NY 10028
(212) 879-5655
A private, nonsectarian organization, this center offers professional counseling services for individuals who have suffered loss of various kinds, including widows, widowers, children who have lost parents, and individuals who have lost significant others (in New York and surrounding states).

The Dougy Center
P.O. Box 86582
Portland, OR 97286
(503) 775-5683
www.dougy.org
e-mail: help@dougy.org
Provides telephone assistance and literature to widowed persons with children and adolescents. Maintains a national directory of children's grief services, which includes referral to resources in caller's local area.

The Eldercare Locator
(800) 677-1116
> A public service of the U.S. Administration on Aging, this is a toll-free number for locating more than 4,800 service providers. Areas of assistance are: adult day care and respite services, nursing home ombudsman assistance, consumer fraud, in-home care complaints, legal services, elder abuse/protective services, Medicaid/Medigap information, tax assistance, and transportation.

National Association for Uniformed Services (NAUS)
Society of Military Widows
5535 Hempstead Way
Springfield, VA 22151-4094
(800) 842-3451
www.naus.org
e-mail: naus@ix.netcom.com
> Call to locate local chapters that help in solving problems for retired military widows, and may provide self-help groups.

National Association of Social Workers
750 First Street NE, Suite 700
Washington, DC 20002-4241
(202) 336-8291
www.socialworkers.org
> Call or visit web site to obtain the names of registered clinical social workers practicing in your local area.

National Council of Senior Citizens
8403 Colesville Rd., Suite 1200
Silver Spring, MD 20910-3314
(888) 373-6467
www.ncscinc.org
e-mail: membership@nscerc.org
> Contact for club or council in your local area. These deal largely with political issues, and most have social components.

National Hospice Organization
1901 North Moore St., Suite 901
Arlington, VA 22209
(800) 658-8898
www.nho.org
e-mail: drsnho@cals.com
   Contact for grief counseling and hospice information.

Parents Without Partners International Headquarters
1650 S. Dixie Hwy., Suite 510
Boca Raton, FL 33432-7461
www.parentswithoutpartners.org
   Provides educational, social, and family services to single parents and their children. General information available.

Recovery, Inc.
802 N. Dearborn St.
Chicago, IL 60610
(312) 337-5661
www.recovery-inc.com
e-mail: spot@recovery-inc.com
   An international organization that uses carefully trained volunteers to lead self-help groups to help persons deal with fears, depression, and stressful situations. No required fee.

SeniorNet
121 Second St., 7th Floor
San Francisco, CA 94105
415-495-4990
www.seniornet.org
   SeniorNet and IBM are working together to help persons over age fifty get on the Internet. IBM is providing computer training and opportunities to buy computing equipment at low prices. The goal is to introduce ten million seniors to the Internet.

SeniorNet has more than 150 learning centers nationwide. Call for one nearest you.

THEOS (They Help Each Other Spiritually)
717 Liberty Avenue, Suite 1301
Pittsburgh, PA 15222
(412) 471-7779
Fax: (412) 471-7782
A national organization assisting newly widowed persons of all ages and their families in the rebuilding of their lives through mutual self-help. Contact them for the location of a group near you.

The Widows'/Widowers' Network
3483 Golden Gate Way Suite #2
Lafayette, CA 94549
(925) 256-7952
www.members.aol.com/wwnwc/wwn.html
e-mail: wwnwc@aol.com
Provides referral to support groups, counseling, and social activities for widowed persons in local areas in U.S.

Women Work! The National Network for Women's Employment
1625 K. Street N.W., Suite 300
Washington, DC 20006
202-467-6346
www.womenwork.org
e-mail: womenwork@womenwork.org
Provides a referral service for locating local programs that retrain and make women employable and, in some cases, offers job referral.

YWCA of the U.S.A.
Empire State Building
350 Fifth Ave., Suite 301
New York, NY 10118

212-273-7800
www.ywca.org/
Under the Displaced Homemakers Act, the YWCA
has government funding to help middle-aged women
enter or reenter the job market. The YMCA also provides educational seminars and programs.

WHERE TO FIND . . .

E

F

G

H

M

Mail detail 36
Marital status 124, 128
Measurement 122, 130, 132, 134, 136
Meditation 20, 26
Memorials 112
Memories 34, 70, 72, 74, 78, 100, 108, 120
Men, how they grieve 102
Messages
    negative 42
    positive 44
    to loved one 76, 82, 90, 108, 110, 112
Monotony 50
Morning 40

N

Naps 38
Nature 92
Needs 14
Night time 38
Nurturing, self 12, 18, 30, 32, 40, 44, 50, 64, 66, 70, 84, 92, 114, 120
Nutrition 32

O

On-line 118
Optimism 40
Organizing 36
Others
    reach out to 104, 106, 116, 118, 126
    responsibility for 56, 58, 60

Marta Felber, author of *Grief Expressed: When a Mate Dies*, has more than forty years of experience in church work, social service, and counseling. Today, Marta enjoys daily walks in the gentle Ozark Mountains surrounding her in Northwest Arkansas.